SPIRITUAL JOURNALING

Recording Your Journey Toward God

A SPIRITUAL FORMATION STUDY GUIDE
BY RICHARD PEACE

NAVPRESS

BRINGING TRUTH TO LIFE
NavPress Publishing Group
P.O. Box 35001, Colorado Springs, Colorado 80935

Visit the NavPress web site at: http://www.navpress.com/

ISBN: 1-57683-109-4

Cover illustration by Wood River Media, Inc., San Rafael, CA

(Originally published in 1995, this edition has been fully revised and
updated.)

Printed in the United States of America

1 2 3 4 5 6 7 8 9 10 / 02 01 00 99 98

FOR A FREE CATALOG OF
NAVPRESS BOOKS & BIBLE STUDIES,
CALL 1-800-366-7788 (USA).
IN CANADA, CALL 1-416-499-4615.

CONTENTS

SPIRITUAL FORMATION STUDY GUIDES
BY RICHARD PEACE

How to Use This Guide

Introduction

For some years I have wanted to write a series of small group study guides focusing on the spiritual disciplines. I have several motives. For one thing, the spiritual disciplines provide an avenue through which we can approach God and learn about God. Such a series could assist us in our spiritual exploration. For another thing, the spiritual disciplines provide a way to spiritual health and maturity. Clearly this is a great need in the church today. Widespread research indicates that there is no distinguishable lifestyle characteristic by which to discern between those who attend church and those who do not. It seems that the teachings of Jesus have not sunk very deeply into his followers.

It also has been clear to me that in this modern, over-active world in which we live our only hope of exploring spiritual disciplines would be in a small group alongside interested others. Hence this series.

As you begin you will need to know that this series is written from the perspective of Christian spirituality. I understand that the spiritual pilgrimage unfolds in different ways for different people. But it is my belief that there is far more value to approaching this topic from a particular spiritual perspective rather than from the vantage point of a vague, lowest-common-denominator spirituality. In any case, my own pilgrimage is all about trying to follow Jesus and so this is what I can write about and this is what I am concerned with.

The series begins with journaling because, apart from anything else, this is the first discipline I explored. I was introduced to journaling in the fall of 1975 when I attended my first Intensive Journal Workshop. This workshop was a profoundly important experience in that it taught me a method of personal and spiritual exploration that has become essential in my own spiritual pilgrimage. I owe a debt of gratitude to Dr. Ira Progoff, whose writings and workshops have significantly affected my life.

Progoff's ideas shine through at various places in this book.

I have not slavishly followed his schema, however. Over the years I have adapted and expanded his materials. In particular, in teaching journaling to hundreds of theological students over the past twenty years, I have tried to develop methods that incorporate the unique elements of Christian spirituality into the journaling process. I am grateful for all that I have learned from these students.

How is the study guide put together?
This study guide is designed to teach you how to journal, either alone or with a small group, in order to further your spiritual pilgrimage.

Each of the eight sessions represents a sixty- to ninety-minute lesson containing the following elements:

❖ *Introduction & Overview:* a reflection on one aspect of spiritual journaling, and a preview of this week's session

❖ *Telling Our Stories:* (for groups) a set of questions that will build relationships among group members and help you begin to think about the topic at hand

❖ *Journaling Method:* an explanation of the method you will use in the session, with particular emphasis on that method's role in fostering spiritual growth

❖ *Journaling Exercise:* instructions for trying out the method either alone or with your group

❖ *Journal Sharing:* (for groups, but also helpful for individuals) questions for discussing what you thought of the journaling exercise and what you learned from it

❖ *Journaling Assignment:* instructions for using the journaling method further during the week

❖ *Journal Reading:* an excerpt from the published journal of a well-known person (to show different styles of personal reflection)

In addition to the material in each of the eight sessions, there is an introductory chapter on the art of journaling and an appendix of notes for use by small group leaders.

You can use this guide on your own simply by skipping the two sections that are for groups only ("Telling Our Stories" and "Journal Sharing"). However, you will find it beneficial if you can get together with two or three other people (or as many as ten) with whom to do the exercises. Journaling in groups is a powerful experience.

There are two sections of homework: "Journaling Assignment" and "Journal Reading."

If you are meeting with a group, you will need a designated leader for each session. You may want to rotate this responsibility, or one person can do it consistently. The leader's job will be to watch the clock, introduce each section, answer the relational questions first (as a model for others), and guide the focusing exercise. The instructions for leading each session are simple and can be found on pages 105-111.

How will journaling benefit me?

Journaling helps us pay attention to God. It is a way of hearing and responding to God.

Journaling helps us understand our unfolding story. Knowing our story helps us to see what God has been doing in the past, is doing now, and is calling us to do in the future.

Is this course designed for church members only?

No—anyone can benefit from it. All that is required is an interest in journaling and a spiritual openness to God. In fact, the small group would be a good experience for anyone just beginning his or her own spiritual journey. The material is written in ordinary language for the most part. When theological terms are used, they are explained.

How long will the study take?

The material is best covered by meeting once a week for eight weeks. Other options include meeting every other week, doing all the sessions in two consecutive half-day Saturday seminars, or doing all the sessions at a weekend retreat.

What kind of small group commitment is involved?
If you meet as a group, each member should agree to attend all eight sessions and to abide by certain ground rules. Ideally, every small group should have a covenant (or contract) among members. Ground rules vary, but here are some typical ones:

❖ *Attendance:* I agree to be at each session unless a genuine emergency arises.

❖ *Participation:* I will enter enthusiastically into group discussion and sharing.

❖ *Confidentiality:* I will not share with anyone outside the group the stories of those in the group.

❖ *Honesty:* I will be forthright and truthful in what is said. If I do not feel I can share something, I will say, "I pass," for that question.

❖ *Openness:* I will be appropriately candid with others.

❖ *Respect:* I will not judge others, give advice, or criticize.

❖ *Care:* I will be appropriately open to the needs of others.

What should I do to get ready for the first session?
Read "The Art of Journaling" (pages 97-103). Here you will find a description of the journaling process and an overview of how a small group functions.

Is it necessary to do the journaling assignment?
You will learn to journal by journaling, so the more time you can spend working in your journal during the week, the better. Some groups will begin each new session with a brief sharing time from the journal entries that were written during the week. Some weeks you may have no time to journal. Even if this is the case you still can attend the group and learn the next method (which you can practice when you have time).

Using a Journal to Capture Your History

YOUR PRESENT PERIOD

A journal is more than a diary; it does not so much record our days as record our spirits.

Group Note:
Are you using this study guide with a group of friends? If so, your experience will be enhanced by appointing a leader from your group. Each week that person will review the Leader's Notes (pages 105-111) ahead of time and facilitate your session accordingly.

Journals have existed in many forms down through the ages. In all likelihood, the earliest journals were oral, not written. A tribe would appoint someone to "remember" its history, and on special occasions, this storyteller would recount the events that made the tribe a unique people.

This was true of the Hebrews. They told their story over and over again, recording it in what is today the Old Testament. Their stories described how God sent their father, Abraham, on a long pilgrimage, how Moses led them out of Egypt through the Red Sea, how they entered the Promised Land, and how they came to have a king. In these stories, the Jews found their identity as a special people.

This was true for the earliest followers of Christ as well. The accounts in the four Gospels are simply written versions of oral stories that had been circulating for years within the believing community. The Gospels are, then, a journal of the early church, recounting what Jesus taught, how he died to atone for the sins of the world, and how he changed the lives of the earliest believers.

Taken together, the Old and New Testaments represent God's use of story to trace the thread of God's relationship with people down through the ages.

We are also familiar with journals kept by individuals. Some were written by famous people—explorers like Sir Richard F. Burton, missionaries like Dr. David Livingstone, and theologians like Augustine. Some of these journals are elegant literary works. Sören Kierkegaard's journal has been called one of the world's great masterpieces. Other journals inspire us. The journals of the famous mathematician and philosopher Blaise Pascal, author of *Pensées*, or John Wesley (founder of the Methodist church) have moved readers to greater devotion and action.

But most journals are written by ordinary men and women. Never intended for anyone else to read, these journals are merely attempts to capture the meaning of a person's life. Compared to the works of Augustine, Pascal, and Wesley, they may not come across as especially profound or spiritually uplifting. However, they have great value for their authors, allowing them to see—over time—their unique journey of faith emerge.

For those who seek to follow Jesus, journals are an ideal way to track their journey and to interact with Jesus along the way. Journals help them to know themselves and God, and to see God at work in the intricacies of their lives.

Session Overview

Effective journaling begins by noticing the larger context of our lives. A good place to start is for you to identify the time frame in which you are currently living, your Present Period. Working with your Present Period will help you recognize the cutting edge of your spiritual life—the issues that confront you and that the Holy Spirit urges you to respond to. Working with your Present Period also will help you understand the particular character of this phase of your life.

If you are using this guide on your own, you are welcome to skip the group exercises ("Telling Our Stories" and "Journal Sharing"). If you are using this guide with a group, you will cover all of the sections from "Telling Our Stories" through "Journal Sharing" during the group meeting, and then you will do the "Journaling Assignment" and "Journal Reading" sections at home.

By the way. . .

The exercise on the next page is designed for group use, so if you are using this guide individually, you may wish to skip directly to the following section. However, if you have the time, it is recommended that you read through the group sections because they will help you think about what to include in your journal.

TELLING OUR STORIES   **15-20 Minutes**

Dear Diary . . .

We may not recognize them as such, but many of our efforts to preserve memories (such as photo albums, diaries, family stories, and e-mail files) are, in fact, forms of journaling. It is useful to examine the process of remembering.

1. a. Introduce yourself to the group by describing what activity demands most of your attention during an average week.

   b. What is one reason you joined this group?

2. In which form(s) does your past exist?

   ❑ in a diary
   ❑ in family stories we still share at reunions
   ❑ in old letters
   ❑ in the memory of someone in my family
   ❑ in a journal
   ❑ in family records
   ❑ in secrets shared with a friend
   ❑ in my memory only
   ❑ in no form that I know of
   ❑ other:

3. a. What experience of journaling (or preserving something of your history) have you had as an adult?

   b. Of what use has this been to you?

JOURNALING METHOD   5 Minutes

The Present Period[1]

Life unfolds in phases. As you look back over time, you will realize that your life consists of a series of distinct periods of time, and each period has its own character.

For example, I look back on my college years and realize that this period had a character quite unlike any time in my life before or since. I had a particular set of friends: roommates, dormmates, classmates. I was engaged in a particular task: getting an education and acquiring the skills I would need in my career. I had certain authority figures that I listened to or reacted against: college professors, authors of the books I read, campus leaders. I lived a particular lifestyle: going to bed very late, eating in a college dining hall, structuring my time around the academic calendar. I reacted in certain ways to national issues. I had particular spiritual and emotional concerns. Clearly college was unlike any other time of my life.

This is true throughout our lives. Life is a series of interconnecting periods of time, and each period has its own distinctive character. So when we seek to understand who we are at any point in time, we must take into account the period in which we are living. Our life at any point is bigger than the moment. Who we are, what we wrestle with, what we cherish, and what motivates us are all connected to the period in which we are living.

Therefore, our journaling must begin with us seeking to understand the nature and character of the period of time in which we are now living, our Present Period.

13

JOURNALING EXERCISE   15-30 Minutes

Preparation

There are two parts to this exercise: *Discerning Your Present Period* and *Defining Your Present Period*.

First, take out your journal and find a comfortable spot for writing. Date your entry, and entitle it "The Present Period."

Next, do the focusing exercise on page 107. (If you are meeting with a group, the leader will guide you in this process.) Your aim at this point is to relax, focus on the topic, and ask the Holy Spirit to lead you as you journal.

Discerning Your Present Period

With your eyes closed, ask yourself this question: *In what period of my life am I now living?*

Then simply notice what images, metaphors, feelings, and thoughts present themselves to you. Record these in your journal. You can write lists of words, clusters of phrases, a stream of consciousness, or sentences. Try to stay focused inward. Do not evaluate what comes to you (you'll do that later on); do not censor your thoughts; do not interpret these images. Instead, be alert not only to thoughts, but to physical sensations, images, and feelings.

Defining Your Present Period

Once you've spent some time *Discerning Your Present Period* you will begin to sense the time frame you are working with. Now the task is to define that period by identifying its distinguishing characteristics. In your journal, answer the following questions:

❖ When did this period of life begin? Identify the *boundary* that separates this period from previous periods. This boundary may be a transition in your life (a new job, a new task, a new relationship), an event (an auto accident, the birth of a child), a new discovery (that you are called to a ministry), or a new decision (to prepare for a new career, to start work on a novel).

❖ Who are the *key people* in your life during this period?

14

What role does each play in your life? Which relationships
are satisfying? Disappointing? Why?

❖ What *distinguishing events* characterize this period of time?
These may be personal or national events. Or, perhaps, the
lack of anything new in your life is a distinguishing characteristic.

❖ What are the *key concepts* that mark this time of life? What
ideas are especially important to you now? What are you
reading about? Thinking about? What interests you? What
concepts are you wrestling with?

❖ What are the *major responsibilities* that characterize this
time period? In other words, how do you spend your time?
What interests you most? Least? What is most creative
about your life in this period? Most demanding?

❖ What characterizes your *inner state* during this period? How
would you describe your prayer life (active, inactive)?
Reflective life? Emotional life?

❖ What is your *physical state* during this period? Are you
healthy? Not too well? What are your health challenges?

You will not have enough time in one sitting to fully explore
your Present Period. That will be your journaling task during
the coming week.

By the way. . .

The exercise on the following page can be used either for group
discussion or individual reflection (to help you focus your
thoughts). If you are using this guide individually, simply respond in
your journal to the questions.

JOURNAL SHARING 20-30 Minutes

When you finish journaling, discuss your findings with the group, sharing at whatever level you are comfortable with. (If you are using this guide individually, simply record your responses in your journal.)

1. Explore the process of journaling:

   a. What was the easiest part of the process for you? Why?

   b. What was the most difficult part of the process for you? Why?

   c. What new thing did you learn about how to journal?

2. Share insights from your journaling experience:

   a. What kinds of thoughts, impressions, experiences, and so on came to you during the *Discerning Your Present Period* exercise?

   b. What is the boundary that marks the beginning of the Present Period for you?

   c. What are some of your key insights into this period?

   d. Describe the character of your Present Period: "These are the _____ years of my life."

3. Pray about this experience. What single thing would you like to pray about, or have the group pray about?

JOURNALING ASSIGNMENT

The best way to learn how to journal is by journaling, so you'll want to set aside time this week to add to your journal. In particular, you should expand your understanding of the Present Period. Some specific things to explore include:

- ❖ key people
- ❖ key events
- ❖ key ideas
- ❖ key responsibilities
- ❖ your inner state
- ❖ your physical state

Ask God to help you understand the key issues in your life and the decisions you are being asked to make during this Present Period.

If you are meeting with a group, decide what you will share from your journal at the next session. Each member will have several minutes to share at the start of the meeting.

Finally, read the excerpt from Henri Nouwen's journal under the following "Journal Reading" section. Each of the journal excerpts in this study guide is included to demonstrate the variety of ways people have used journaling to chronicle and cultivate their spiritual journeys.

JOURNAL READING

One of the better known contemporary journals is Henri J. M. Nouwen's *The Genesee Diary: Report from a Trappist Monastery*. In it he describes his seven-month stay in a monastery, where he wrestled with various questions about his relationship with God.

My desire to live for seven months in a Trappist Monastery, not as a guest but as a monk, did not develop overnight. It was the outcome of many years of restless searching. While teaching, lecturing, and writing about the importance of solitude, inner freedom, and peace of mind, I kept stumbling over my own compulsions and illusions. What was driving me from one book to another, one place to another, one project to another? What made me think and talk about "the reality of the Unseen" with the seriousness of one who had seen all that is real? What was turning my vocation to be a witness to God's love into a tiring job? These questions kept intruding themselves into my few unfilled moments and challenging me to face my restless self. Maybe I spoke more about God than with him. Maybe my writing about prayer kept me from a prayerful life. Maybe I was more concerned about the praise of men and women than the love of God. Maybe I was slowly becoming a prisoner of people's expectations instead of a man liberated by divine promises. Maybe . . . it was not all that clear, but I realized that I would only know by stepping back and allowing the hard questions to touch me even if they hurt. . . .

While realizing my growing need to step back, I knew that I could never do it alone. It seems that the crucial decisions and the great experiences of life require a guide. The way to "God alone" is seldom traveled alone.

About ten years ago, while on a long trip from Miami to Topeka, I stopped at the Trappist Abbey of Gethsemani in Kentucky, in the hope of finding someone with whom I could talk. When the guestmaster learned that I had studied psychology and was at the point of joining the faculty of a psychology department, he said with a happy twinkle in his eyes: "But we Trappists have a psychologist too! I will ask him to visit you." A little later Father John Eudes Bamberger walked into the guest room. Very soon I knew that I had met a rare and very convincing person. John Eudes listened to me with care and interest, but also with a deep convic-

tion and a clear vision; he gave me much time and attention but did not allow me to waste a minute; he left me fully free to express my feelings and thoughts but did not hesitate to present his own; he offered me space to deliberate about choices and to make decisions but did not withhold his opinion that some choices and decisions were better than others; he let me find my own way but did not hide the map that showed the right direction. In our conversation, John Eudes emerged not only as a listener but also as a guide, not only as a counselor but also as a director. It did not take me long to realize that this was the man I had needed so badly.

Finally on June 1, 1974, after a lot of desk cleaning, I flew to Rochester, New York, to live as a Trappist monk for seven months, and on Pentecost, June 2, I started to write the notes that found their final form in this diary.[2]

Notes

1. This concept (which Dr. Ira Progoff calls the Now Period) and others which follow, are taken from his seminal work (as described in his many books and in his Intensive Journal Workshops). I did my first Intensive Journal Workshop in the fall of 1975. It was a profoundly important experience in that it taught me a method of personal and spiritual exploration that I have used in my spiritual pilgrimage. I owe a profound debt of gratitude to Dr. Progoff.

2. Henri J. M. Nouwen, *The Genesee Diary: Report from a Trappist Monastery* (Garden City, NY: Image Books, Doubleday, 1976), pp. 13-16.

Using a Journal to Understand the Present

YOUR DAILY LOG

It takes so much time to live my life that I have no time left for writing my life.

Group Note: Leader's Notes for this session can be found on page 108.

Journals help us make sense of our lives. They cause us to notice what is happening to us—and in us—each day. They also allow us to respond to these realities.

So much happens every day. It has been estimated that the average American adult is exposed to over 16,000 separate sensory impressions each day. How do we notice all this, make sense out of it, or respond to it? Mostly, we don't notice and we don't respond. The result is that we drift through life rather than take hold of it.

When we open a journal and record memories and images of the previous twenty-four hours, we begin to take charge of our lives. More specifically, journals help us:

❖ *Identify the significant events of each day.* Not all that happens to us is noteworthy. In each day there are important ideas, feelings, decisions, actions, temptations, relationships, experiences, and spiritual events that shape us. Journals help us notice.

❖ *Respond to what we discover.* We do not have complete control over our lives, but we can make decisions about what

21

we accept and what we reject, about what we will and
won't be like. Journals help us make decisions that promote growth.

❖ *Order our scattered impressions.* For most of us, life is like
an MTV video—all sorts of things are happening, flung at
us rapidly in small doses. What does it all mean? Who
are we in the midst of all this input? Journals help us
make sense of what's happening to us.

❖ *Listen to God.* God is alive and present always, but we
miss many signs of God's presence if we don't pay attention. Journals help us notice God.

Journals enable us to move from fog to clarity; to see, feel, and
live. It is much easier to live in the past (through memories) or
in the future (through fantasies) than to live in the present
(through each moment). Journals make the present come alive.

To be a follower of Christ is to live in the present moment.
It is a life with God: to seek God, to hear God, to respond to
God, to worship and love God, and to obey God. Journals
therefore become a vital tool for living in the present with God.

Session Overview
In this session, you will learn how to keep a Daily Log, and use
this log to examine the past twenty-four hours of your life.

The Daily Log provides a format to help you notice the
presence of God in each day, as well as to respond to what God
is saying to you. Over time, this log provides a record of the
key events in your life which, when reviewed, gives you a reading on the character and direction of your life.

By the way. . .
The exercise on the next page is designed for group use, so if you
are using this guide individually, you may wish to skip directly to
the following section. However, if you have the time, it is recommended that you read through the group sections because they
will help you think about what to include in your journal.

TELLING OUR STORIES   **15-20 Minutes**

From now on you have a choice of how to begin each session. You can use questions 1-3 below, or you can share insights from each person's journaling during the previous week. If you decide to share insights from journaling, go around the circle and give each person a chance to share briefly. Limit each person's sharing to two minutes so that you save enough time for the rest of the session.

Life is such a rush . . .
For most of us, the problem is *not* finding things to do; it's finding time to do all the things we want (and need) to do.

1. Describe your typical weekday morning. What is the most hectic part of the morning for you? The most relaxed?

2. How do you cope with daily pressure?

   ❏ exercise   ❏ make jokes about it
   ❏ meditate   ❏ think positively
   ❏ sleep   ❏ explode
   ❏ daydream   ❏ I don't cope
   ❏ pray   ❏ keep going
   ❏ quit   ❏ what pressure?
   ❏ other:

3. If time and money were no problem, which of the following would you most like to do? Why?

   ❏ travel around the world
   ❏ build a dream house
   ❏ learn gourmet cooking
   ❏ collect folk art
   ❏ write a novel
   ❏ race Formula One cars
   ❏ paint seascapes of all the oceans
   ❏ other:

JOURNALING METHOD   5 Minutes
The Daily Log

The most common use of a journal is to record and respond to the events of a day. This is the journal as diary. Here you write down the stuff of your life: the special things that happen, who you met, what you said, how you felt, the challenges you faced, your emotional tone that day, and so on.

In your Daily Log you record not just what happened, but how you processed it. In fact, the "how" is generally more significant than the "what." For example, you meet a friend in the hall. You chat for a few minutes. Later, when you note the event in your Daily Log, you remember the tension you felt. You weren't especially happy to see your friend, but you didn't say anything. You ended the conversation quickly with an excuse about getting to a meeting. You remember the hurt look on her face. As you remember all of this, you ask yourself, *What's going on?* And so you begin to identify previously unacknowledged stress in an important relationship. The Daily Log allows you to process events from an *internal* perspective.

The Daily Log also allows you to process events from a *spiritual* perspective. After identifying a problem in your relationship, it is natural to pray about it right away: "Lord, what's going on here? Lori is a good friend. Help me to see the issue. Help me to be a good friend to her." Write out your prayer. And once you have prayed, listen. You asked God a question, so sit in silence. Be open to God. You may get some insight into the situation. Or you may remember a passage from Philippians, which you check out. Or you may move on to the next step in journaling, while keeping the question you asked in the back of your mind.

A log is a record of progress. In your Daily Log, you keep track of your life's unfolding. When scanned as a whole, your log becomes a useful picture of where you have come from, where you are now, and where you seem to be heading.

You might also consider recording your dreams. Dreams can reveal what is going on inside you at a subconscious level. Recording them is simply extending the Daily Log into your sleeping hours. The point of dreams is not to discover some direct hotline to God and avoid the normal means of Scripture, prayer, and meditation. While God can (and does) sometimes speak to people in dreams, our intention at this point is to discover what our dreams say about us. By recording dreams in addition to the key elements of our day (activities, relationships, ideas, happenings, feelings, physical experiences, and spiritual events), we can review them to discern important themes and gain new insights. We will return to the topic of dreams in session six.

JOURNALING EXERCISE   **15-30 Minutes**

Preparation

First, take out your journal and find a comfortable spot for writing. Date your entry and entitle it "Daily Log."

Next, do the focusing exercise on page 107, asking the Holy Spirit to lead you as you journal (if you are meeting with a group, the leader will guide you in this process). Once you have relaxed and focused, begin journaling in silence for the time allotted.

Exercise

In this two-part exercise we're going to explore the previous twenty-four hours of your life. Our aim is not to write every detail of the past twenty-four hours, but to pinpoint the key elements of the past day, whether activities, relationships, ideas, happenings, dreams, feelings, physical experiences, or spiritual events.

Begin by creating a Daily Log. Recall how you spent the major blocks of time in the past twenty-four hours: What did you do yesterday evening? What was last night's sleep like? How did you spend your morning and afternoon? In other words, identify the character of the past day.

Next, recall the details of each block of time. In each time block, identify the following:

❖ *Major events:* what you worked on, where you went, what you did, what you watched and listened to, and the other activities of the past twenty-four hours

❖ *Key relationships:* whom you met, how you interacted, what you felt, what you said, the state of your various relationships

❖ *Important ideas:* the ideas that caught your attention or troubled you, intrigued you, baffled you, amused you, or challenged you (note where you encountered these ideas and how they fit—or didn't fit—into your worldview)

❖ *External happenings in the world around you:* major news stories, local events, incidents at work

❖ *Internal happenings in the world within you:* dreams, sensations, intuitions, creative responses

❖ *Strongest feelings:* positive (happiness, joy, excitement, contentment, hope) and negative (depression, bitterness, discouragement, disappointment, guilt, fear, anger, indifference)

❖ *Notable physical experiences:* how you felt, any exercise you had, headaches or other ailments, what you ate and drank, the sexual side of your life

❖ *Spiritual events:* your experience in prayer, Bible study, worship, and other spiritual disciplines; the sense of God's presence

❖ *Conclusions reached:* your assessment of the day, the choices you made, your responses, questions you are left with

Use this checklist to find out where the focus of your day was. In most cases it will have been dominated by one or two of these categories. Explore them, paying particular attention to the conclusions you reached—some of which you may not have been conscious of at the time. As you journal, you may find yourself making new decisions. In other words, notice and interact with your previous day.

By the way. . .
The exercise on the following page can be used either for group discussion or individual reflection (to help you focus your thoughts). If you are using this guide individually, simply respond in your journal to the questions.

JOURNAL SHARING   20-30 Minutes

When you finish journaling, discuss your findings with the group, record them in your journal, or discuss them with a close friend.

1. Explore the process of journaling:

   a. What was the easiest part of the process for you? Why?

   b. What was the most difficult part of the process for you? Why?

   c. What new thing did you learn about how to journal?

2. Share your insights from the journal experience:

   a. What did you discover about the structure of your day when you took the time to keep a Daily Log?

   b. As you scanned the past twenty-four hours with respect to the various categories, which one(s) dominated your day? How? Why?

   c. What was your key insight from the past twenty-four hours?

   d. What conclusions did you reach about your day?

3. Pray about this experience. What single thing would you like to pray about, or have the group pray about?

JOURNALING ASSIGNMENT

During the coming week reread the material in this session, including the following "Journal Reading" excerpt from *Conversations with God: The Devotional Journals of Myrtie L. Elmer.*

Also, practice working with your Daily Log by doing at least three daily entries during the week. Remember to explore your days by examining:

* ❖ major events
* ❖ key relationships
* ❖ important ideas
* ❖ external happenings
* ❖ internal happenings
* ❖ strongest feelings
* ❖ notable physical experiences
* ❖ spiritual events
* ❖ conclusions reached

Ask God to help you understand the key issues in your life at this time. Take note of issues you currently are wrestling with. Discern new insights you have into your unfolding story.

If you are meeting with a group (or a close friend), decide what parts of your Daily Log you want to share the next time you meet. Remember that you will have only a few minutes. Share things that will help others know you—perhaps exciting or new discoveries. Be willing to be appropriately open with the group in what you share.

JOURNAL READING

Myrtie Elmer began writing in a journal at age seventy-eight. She did so at the urging of her pastor, Raymond Gibson, though she felt it presumptuous. But this feeling changed. Early in the process she wrote, "This book was begun in obedience to an impulse so strong that, feeling it to be possible there might be a reason for it, I could not willingly disregard it."[1]

Gibson urged her to write because in his many conversations with her he felt the "sense of the presence of God." It was not that she was some sort of saint. In fact, her life had been simple in the extreme. What he saw in Myrtie (I think) was the fruition of a life of faithful devotion to God. A lot of published journals come from the pens of great leaders such as Teresa or Augustine. Myrtie Elmer is a lot more like all of us—and it is encouraging that Eerdmans saw fit to publish the journals of a woman who lived simply and trusted God daily.

September 15, 1953
How I wish I had the ability to make the words that I wish to speak come alive. When I want to express the deep yearning of my heart words seem so lacking in meaning and intensity. The feeling lies hidden in my own heart.

August 10
I should like to make my prayer tonight this one by St. Augustine:

> *"Grant me, even me, my dearest Lord, to know Thee and love Thee and rejoice in Thee. And, if I cannot do this perfectly in this life, let me at least advance to higher degrees every day till I can come to do them to perfection.*
>
> *"Let the knowledge of Thee increase in me here that it may be full hereafter. Let the love of Thee grow every day more and more here that it may be perfect hereafter; that my joy may be great in itself and full in Thee.*
>
> *"I know, O God, that Thou art a God of truth; O make good Thy gracious promises to me that my joy may be full. Amen."*

August 22
My Heavenly Father, each time this morning when I have gone into

the wonderful out-of-doors and have looked up into the beautiful blue sky, I have seen and felt, not only its beauty and majestic peace, but also have known in my heart the graciousness and love of the Creator of the universe—even Thyself, O God—and Thy Holy Spirit has brought peace and joy.

September 14
Almighty and Eternal God, I give Thee thanks that in the hours of pain and discomfort Thou dost not leave me, for I need the comfort of Thy presence.

September 15
The report of the doctor today was not easy to take as the outlook is filled with foreboding and dread. [Her doctor had just told her she might lose her sight.] *It is hard for me to pray tonight. Not that I do not feel my need of Thee nor that I doubt Thy mercy and care through all that lies ahead, but I don't seem to know how to pray as I should. Thou knowest the hidden fear in my heart. If it can be right in accordance with Thy will, let not that fear be real-ized—not so much fear of death as of the cause.*

I have longed tonight for someone else to pray for me. Dear Jesus, wilt Thou intercede for me as I pray in Thy name? As another night of pain begins, give courage and strength to meet it, dear Lord.

September 19
Thou great and infinite God, when I think of Thy majesty and power I am filled with awe, and yet that is the spirit in which I come, for I know Thou art not far from me.

I thank Thee most reverently that through Thy grace I am assured that whatever the future may hold for me, all is well, so long as I do nothing to thwart Thy divine purpose. Thou has brought a peace which is helping me to be able to pray again, and with a deeper faith and trust. Grant that my prayer may be, not for relief from suffering of any kind, except insofar as is best in Thy sight, but rather for strength from Thee to replace my weak-ness. Forgive the hours of weakness. Forgive the too-great anxiety over temporal concerns or even over trivialities which has often filled my heart to such a degree as to lessen my ability to praise

Thy name. Let tension or worry never close my heart or mind to the influence of Thy guiding Spirit.

October 8
Day after day, as I live my life, performing the necessary daily tasks, attending to business calls, and all the trivial incidental matters, I often wonder if I am doing anything worthwhile for God except to love and adore him and worship him. I had hoped that I might be able to show forth his Spirit, not by words, but by the grace inspired by communion with him in my contacts with others. But I see comparatively few, and then I think I do not make the right amount of effort. May God help me to overcome too great diffidence and self-consciousness. God grant that I may not waste either time or opportunities![2]

Notes
1. Raymond E. Gibson, ed., *Conversations with God: The Devotional Journals of Myrtie L. Elmer* (Grand Rapids, MI: Eerdmans, 1962), p. vi.
2. *Conversations with God*, pp. 15-17.

Using a Journal to Recover Your Past

HINGE EVENTS

There are vivid memories to be sure, but there are also dark gaps. It is in those gaps I must look to understand who I am.

Group Note:
Leader's Notes for this session can be found on page 109.

John Calvin begins his influential work, *Institutes of the Christian Religion*, with the statement that true wisdom has two parts: knowledge of God and knowledge of self. As followers of Christ, we turn to the Bible in our search to know God. But what about the search to know ourselves? This is where journals come in. They not only facilitate a daily awareness of who we are becoming, but also help us probe the past to know who we've been.

This is a vital task if we are to discern clearly the main lines in the story of our spiritual pilgrimage. We cannot really know who we are now—much less who we will become—unless we know who we were as a child, a teenager, a young adult, a newlywed, and so on.

But how do we lay hold of the past? It is often quite murky. We forget so much. And what we do remember is not always reliable. In his journaling workshops, Dr. Ira Progoff suggests that we treat our past not as a single and undifferentiated whole, but as a series of interconnected periods. Each period has its own character and yields its own data about who we were at that point in time.

Of course, it would have been helpful if we had kept detailed journals beginning when we first learned to write, but few of us have done that. In any case, they merely would show how we understood ourselves at that time. This, of course, would not have been fully accurate. The way we now assess our turbulent adolescent years is quite different from what we understood when we went through them. Progoff argues that what we need to know is our history from an internal point of view—not just the "facts," but what the people, events, ideas, and emotions meant to us in each period of time.

For some of us, examining the past may be difficult. There may be painful memories or broken relationships we'd rather leave alone. But even though it may be hard to probe the pain of the past, it is important to do so. In fact, the present can be the *best* time to examine these things, for as time passes the pain loses some of its sting. We also mature, which gives us a better vantage point from which to explore and understand what happened.

By reviewing our past, we also begin to recognize the footprints of God in our life. They weren't always clear at the time, but in retrospect we can see patterns. We come to understand how God was at work, shaping us in unique ways. And so we understand our story from a spiritual—as well as historical— point of view.

Session Overview

A hinge is a turning point when life moves from one direction to another. Generally, hinge events are not dramatic—for example, moving fifty miles to start a new job. But in retrospect we see that life changed because of that move.

In this session you will identify a series of hinge-points in your life and see how they mark the periods of your life. Identifying these periods will help you discover your story and see the ways in which God has been at work.

TELLING OUR STORIES   15-20 Minutes

Memories . . .

The ability to remember is a great gift because in this way we can relive the high points in our lives.

1. Which period of time was the most fun for you? Which was the most challenging? Explain your choices.

   ❑ grade school
   ❑ high school
   ❑ college
   ❑ my twenties
   ❑ my thirties
   ❑ mid-life
   ❑ my fifties
   ❑ retirement
   ❑ other:

2. Pick one of the categories below and describe a great experience or event connected to it:

   ❑ special vacations
   ❑ fun accomplishments
   ❑ historic events
   ❑ unforgettable meals
   ❑ great gatherings
   ❑ meaningful milestones
   ❑ memorable moments
   ❑ aesthetic experiences

3. If you could arrange a memorable event for you and your family, what would you do?

JOURNALING METHOD   5 Minutes
Hinges

The first step in examining the past is to divide your life into a series of time periods that make sense to you. In this exercise, you are looking for transitional events or Hinges—actions, ideas, experiences, or encounters that moved your life in new directions. For example, you leave home for the first time at eighteen to attend a college six hundred miles away; going to college marks a shift in your life and so qualifies as a hinge event. Or you have an auto accident in which you break both legs; the accident launches a new phase in which you learn about dependence and pain. Marriage almost always qualifies as a transitional event, as does conversion or induction into the armed services.

Certain types of events often turn out to be hinge incidents.

❖ *A move from one place to another*: away from your child-hood home; to a new city, state, or country; to a new job; to a new challenge

❖ *A new person in your life*: a spouse, a child, a mentor, a friend, an enemy, a boss, an employee, a relative, a pastor

❖ *A new phase of education*: grade school, middle school, high school, college, graduate school, seminary, profes-sional seminars

❖ *A new commitment*: marriage, birth of a child, joining a church, beginning a business, taking out a mortgage

❖ *A traumatic incident*: death of a loved one, an accident or illness, unexpected success or failure, loss of a job

❖ *A religious experience*: conversion, an answer to prayer, a mystical encounter, a retreat, a worship experience, a small group

❖ *A national event*: a war, a recession, new legislation, death of a leader or hero, a shift in national perception

❖ *A new idea*: about truth, reality, or morality; encounter with a book, film, or piece of music; experiencing a new group, culture, or discipline

❖ *A creative venture*: beginning to write poetry, to play the saxophone, or to read biographies; starting a journal or a potter's shop; taking up photography or exploring back roads

When you have defined these hinges, you have divided your life into a series of periods. The challenge, then, is to begin to understand the character of the time periods *between* hinge events. What did you become in that period, and how has it made you who you are today? In particular, you need to recall the following for each period:

❖ the key people
❖ the activities or responsibilities that demanded time and energy
❖ the important ideas
❖ the nature of your inner life: dreams, images, longings, and emotions
❖ the nature of your health: exercise, sport, diet, and illness
❖ the creative impulses that shaped you
❖ the external events that shaped you: events on the national, state, and local scene and their impact on you; the nature of your personal environment

There is no single or correct way to divide your life. In fact, if you did this exercise again in a few years, your hinges would probably be different. You would find some events on both lists, but other events would emerge as crucial. It all depends on your point of view as you look back on your life.

JOURNALING EXERCISE   **15-30 Minutes**

Preparation

There are three parts to this exercise: *Identifying Your Hinge Events, Arranging Your Hinge Events,* and *Describing a Time Period.*

To begin, first take out your journal and find a comfortable spot for writing. Date your entry, and entitle it "Hinges." (If you are organizing your journal into categories, file this exercise in the History section.)

Next, do the focusing exercise on page 107. (If you are meeting with a group, the leader will guide you in this process.) Your aim at this point is to relax, focus on the topic, and ask the Holy Spirit to lead you as you journal.

Identifying Your Hinge Events

With your eyes closed, ask yourself this question: *What are the hinge events in my life?*

Start your list with the entry, "Birth," and then write down the eight to twelve events of your life (these numbers are important) that spontaneously present themselves to you. Don't think too hard about finding events, and don't worry about arranging them in proper order. Just relax and, in an attitude of prayer, open yourself to the ideas that come to you. At this point, do not evaluate what you write (you will work with this material at a later point in the exercise); do not censor your thoughts; do not interpret these images; instead, simply be alert to them.

Arranging Your Hinge Events

Go back over your list of hinge events and put them in chronological order, adding any descriptive phrases that occur to you about the time period that follows the hinge event.

Describing a Time Period

Begin working with one of these time periods. It doesn't matter which one (though you will probably be drawn to one of the hinge events and the period that follows). Using the categories in the Present Period exercise (session one, pages 14-15), describe the period by writing: "It was a time when. . . ."

Describe the important people, distinguishing events, key concepts, major responsibilities, your inner state, your physical
state, and any spiritual events. You will not have enough time
to explore fully the period you have chosen. That will be your
journaling task this week. In fact, it will be your task over the
next months to explore each period in this way, as you seek to
understand your story and see God's hand in it.

JOURNAL SHARING   20-30 Minutes

When you finish journaling, discuss your findings with the
group, record them in your journal, or discuss them with a
close friend.

1. Explore the process of journaling:

   a. What was the easiest part of the process for you? Why?

   b. What was the most difficult part for you? Why?

   c. What new thing did you learn about how to journal?

2. Share your insights from the journal experience:

   a. What are some of the hinge events in your life? Which
      events on this list surprised you? Which events were
      obvious?

   b. Which time period stands out as special or significant for
      you now as you explore your history? Explain.

   c. What new insights did you glean about your past?

   d. In what ways did this exercise challenge you?

3. Pray about this experience. What single thing would you
   like to pray about, or have the group pray about?

JOURNALING ASSIGNMENT

During the coming week, set aside some time to read over all the material in this session, including the following excerpt from *The Journal of John Wesley*.

Pick a particular time period to explore, using the following categories suggested in this week's exercise to help you gain insight:

- ❖ important people
- ❖ distinguishing events
- ❖ key concepts
- ❖ major responsibilities
- ❖ your inner state
- ❖ your physical state
- ❖ spiritual events

Ask God to help you understand the key issues in your life during this period. In what ways was God present in your life then? What new insights do you have into your unfolding story? What is the shape and character of your spiritual pilgrimage during this period?

Decide what you want to share with your group during the next session from your period exploration. Remember that you will have only a few minutes. Share things that will help the group know you better. Share exciting or new discoveries for you. Be willing to be appropriately open with the group in what you share.

JOURNAL READING

John Wesley wrote two journals. One he intended to publish (*The Journal of John Wesley*); the other, which he called his diary, was private. Wesley drew from his private diary in the preparation of his public journal. Wesley's journal ranged far and wide in the subjects it covered. Still, at its heart, it is a vivid description of the work of God in the lives of various men and women. Wesley describes here a critical hinge event for him—the fear that his beloved brother was dying—which ultimately led to a new understanding of faith that transformed his ministry.

Tuesday
I saw my mother once more. The next day I prepared for my journey to my brother at Tiverton. But on Thursday morning, March 2nd, a message that my brother Charles was dying at Oxford, obliged me to set out for that place immediately. Calling at an odd house [an out-of-the-way house] in the afternoon, I found several persons there who seemed well-wishers to religion to whom I spake plainly; as I did in the evening, both to the servants and strangers at my inn.

With regard to my own behavior, I now renewed and wrote down my former resolutions.

1. *To use absolute openness and unreserve, with all I should converse with.*

2. *To labor after continual seriousness, not willingly indulging myself in the least levity of behavior, or in laughter—no, not for a moment.*

3. *To speak no word which does not tend to the glory of God; in particular, not to talk of worldly things. Others may, nay, must. But what is that to thee? And,*

4. *To take no pleasure which does not tend to the glory of God; thanking God every moment for all I do take, and therefore rejecting every sort and degree of it, which I feel I cannot so thank him in and for.*

Saturday
I found my brother at Oxford, recovering from his pleurisy; and with him Peter Böhler; by whom (in the hand of the great God) I was, on Sunday, the 5th, clearly convinced of unbelief, of the want of that faith whereby alone we are saved.

Immediately it struck into my mind, "Leave off preaching. How can you preach to others, who have not faith yourself?" I asked Böhler, whether he thought I should leave it off or not. He said, "Preach faith till you have it; and then, because you have it, you will preach faith."

Monday
Accordingly, I began preaching this new doctrine, though my soul started back from the work. The first person to whom I offered salvation by faith alone, was a prisoner under sentence of death. His name was Clifford. Peter Böhler had many times desired me to speak to him before. But I could not prevail on myself so to do; being still (as I had been many years) a zealous assertor of the impossibility of a death-bed repentance. . . . [1]

Note
1. John Wesley, *The Journal of John Wesley: A Selection*, ed. Elisabeth Jay (Oxford: Oxford University Press, 1987), pp. 27-28.

Using a Journal to Interact with Your History

DIALOGUE

*How did our relationship come unstuck?
What can I do to reconnect?*

Group Note:
Leader's Notes for this session can be found on page 110.

The past is past. It is over and done with. And yet, there is a way in which the past still lives on. It lives through us in terms of what we have become as a result of it. We bear the fruits of the past. Choices we made, actions we undertook, ideas we believed, and relationships we experienced all live on in us—for good and ill.

There are things from the past we wish we could change. On one level, we cannot undo what has been done. But on another, the interior level, we can enter into a new relationship with the past.

For example, John's father was abusive. John remembers the atmosphere of fear in his childhood home. There was one incident in particular that summed up all of his feelings growing up. He came home late one night, thirty-five minutes past curfew. He was dependent on a friend for a ride, and his friend wouldn't leave the party. John's father was waiting for him. John expected the lecture that he got—the cursing, the threats, the demeaning comments. What he didn't expect was the destruction. His father punished him by trashing his room (his safe haven) while John watched. His father ripped the posters off the wall and broke the records he had so carefully collected. Even though John is grown now with a family of his own, he still feels torn up inside whenever he thinks of that night.

John needs to establish a new relationship with this incident, and his journal can help him to do so. First, the journal allows him to recall and write out in great detail the whole event. Often the act of making memories concrete robs them of some of their power over us. We bring them from the darkness into the light.

Second, in his journal John can offer this incident to God in prayer and ask for healing. He can pray a prayer in which, in his imagination, he asks Jesus to stand with him on that fateful night, to be with him as he endures his father's shouts and as his father vents his rage on his room. We cannot always predict where such prayers of imagination will take us, but it is not uncommon for great healing to emerge from them.

Third, in his journal John can begin a dialogue with his father. This journaling method has great power to give us new insight into a relationship and to bring progress to stalled relationships.

It is not just relationships from the past that we must deal with. As you work with the various periods in your life, be on the lookout for any incidents, events, ideas, or behaviors that are still vivid. Where guilt, pain, or questions emerge, that is where our attention should be.

Session Overview

Growth involves dealing with the past so that you move beyond it into wholeness. As you explore your past in your period work, you will come across issues that need resolution. In this session, you will learn how to engage these issues directly by means of a journaled Dialogue. In so doing, you will often receive insight as to what is required in the present to defuse (or grow beyond) the past.

TELLING OUR STORIES   **15-20 Minutes**

People who need people . . .

Life is about relationship. We all have certain relationships that bring light and joy into our lives.

1. When you were a child, who was your best friend? Describe him or her.

2. In what ways was your best friend as a preteen different from your best friend in high school or college?

3. What do you think are the two or three most important characteristics of a best friend?

   ❏ a sense of humor
   ❏ common sense
   ❏ loyalty
   ❏ a sympathetic ear
   ❏ an uncomplaining spirit
   ❏ a fun spirit
   ❏ a deep faith
   ❏ an undemanding nature
   ❏ always available
   ❏ common interests
   ❏ unconditional acceptance and love
   ❏ other:

JOURNALING METHOD   5 Minutes

Dialogue

If our aim is to understand our past relationships, we need a concrete way to observe them. This is what the dialogue method of journaling provides for us.

The idea is simple: we frame an imaginary dialogue with a person. We "talk" to that person in our journal, writing out our conversation. In so doing, we come to a new understanding of our relationship with that person. This is not a mysterious process. We know from experience that in conversation we work out our questions, we sort through our ideas until they are clear, and we realize things that we had not been aware of. Journal dialogues work in the same way.

Imagination can be a powerful tool for growth. Some people worry about the imagination—they believe it is inferior to the intellect and that it cannot be trusted. They forget that our imagination is as much a gift from God as our intellect. And both intellect and imagination can be put to good use or bad; both can be distorted. It depends on how we use them. God intended us to use both.

We can dialogue not only with people, but also with any aspect of our lives. Since this is an imaginary reconstruction anyway, it's possible to imagine a dialogue with our career ("Okay, you and I have got to talk because from my point of view, you are going nowhere . . ."). We can dialogue with incidents that have taken place in the world around us, with our bodies—we can dialogue with anything. The idea may sound strange, but you will be amazed at the insights that emerge. These dialogues work, I am convinced, not because they mystically put us in touch with real entities, but because they allow us to honestly and frankly access thoughts and feelings from our unconscious. Dialogue categories include:

❖ *Persons:* past and present, living and dead, close or distant

❖ *Projects to which you have given energy:* creative works, a job or career, a business venture, a ministry

46

❖ *Body* (the physical side of life): injuries or illness, body parts, our size or shape, physical activities

❖ *Events:* things that happen to us, for good or ill, personal or societal

❖ *Inner realities:* dreams, emotions, values, our attitude toward God, spiritual experiences

❖ *Ideas:* those that grip us, move us, annoy us, challenge us

It is also useful to record our ordinary dialogue. You recall an important conversation during the day. Recording it (or snatches of it) in your journal allows you to reflect on the conversation. In your journal, you can try to extend the conversation or move it in a new direction through this dialogue technique—out of which new clarity may come.

JOURNALING EXERCISE   **15-30 Minutes**

Preparation

There are four parts to this exercise: *Selecting a Dialogue Partner, Describing Your Relationship, Engaging in Dialogue,* and *Reading What you've Written.* You can use this process to dialogue with people, events, projects, ideas, or whatever you think would be most helpful.

To begin, take out your journal and find a comfortable spot for writing. Date your entry, and entitle it "Dialogue." (If you are organizing your journal into categories, file this exercise in the Dialogue section.)

Next, do the focusing exercise on page 107. (If you are meeting with a group, the leader will guide you in this process.) Your aim at this point is to relax, focus on the topic, and ask the Holy Spirit to lead you as you journal.

Selecting a Dialogue Partner

Select a person with whom to dialogue. Pick someone who matters to you, someone with whom you have an association, like a parent or an ex-friend who let you down. Choose a relationship in your past or present that needs a further step of development.

Describing Your Relationship

Describe the present state of your relationship in two to four paragraphs.

> ❖ What is positive about it? Negative?
> ❖ What is open? Hidden?
> ❖ What are its joys? Frustrations?
> ❖ Where does it now stand?

In preparing these paragraphs, you may want to read over past journal entries connected to this relationship.

Engaging in Dialogue

Enter into dialogue with the person. You do this by sitting in silence and imagining that you are with the person (or entity, if your dialogue partner is not a person). Begin a conversation in your mind. Listen to the response. Let the dialogue proceed. Write down the dialogue script as it unfolds. Record it without assessing what is said, while you remain in the imaginary dialogue. Your main focus needs to be on the dialogue, not on interpreting it.

Reading What you've Written

Read over (aloud if possible) the dialogue script. As you do so, note your reactions and assessments in your journal.

- ❖ What new things can you learn about this relationship?
- ❖ What feelings are evoked?
- ❖ What challenges to action are here?
- ❖ What is the next step in your relationship?
- ❖ How must you pray about this relationship?

JOURNAL SHARING   **20-30 Minutes**
When you finish journaling, discuss your findings with the group, record them in your journal, or discuss them with a close friend.

1. Explore the process of journaling:

   a. What was the easiest part of the process for you? Why?

   b. What was the most difficult part of the process for you? Why?

   c. What new thing did you learn about how to journal?

2. Share your insights from the journal experience:

   a. With whom—or what—did you dialogue (and why)?

   b. What are some of the things you learned from the dialogue?

   c. What new insights came from this process that you had not known or considered before?

   d. How easy or difficult was the dialogue exercise for you? How else might you apply it?

3. Pray about this experience. What single thing would you like to pray about, or have the group pray about?

JOURNALING ASSIGNMENT

Allocate some time during the coming week to read over all the
material in this session, including the following excerpt from
Confessions by Saint Augustine.

Use the dialogue method to investigate other aspects of the
time period you have been exploring.

Ask God to bring new insight into your life as a result of
doing these dialogues. Pray that you will be able to apply what
you learn.

Discern new insights you have into your unfolding story.
What new things have you learned about the shape and character of your spiritual pilgrimage during the period you are
exploring?

Decide what you want to share with your group during the
next session from your dialogue exercises.

JOURNAL READING

Saint Augustine's *Confessions* is regarded as one of the greatest
journals in print and as a masterpiece of Western literature.
The title has a double meaning: confession as praise to God
(Augustine's words in this journal are addressed to God) and
confession as admission of faults. Augustine is disarmingly candid about his life. He is amazed when he considers the ways
God has been active in his life. What follows is a famous
excerpt: the account of his conversion.

28

*From a hidden depth a profound self-examination had dredged up
a heap of all my misery and set it "in the sight of my heart"
(Ps. 18:15). That precipitated a vast storm bearing a massive
downpour of tears. To pour it all out with the accompanying groans,
I got up from beside Alypius (solitude seemed to me more appropriate for the business of weeping), and I moved further away to
ensure that even his presence put no inhibition upon me. He sensed
that this was my condition at that moment. I think I may have said
something which made it clear that the sound of my voice was
already choking with tears. So I stood up while in profound aston-
ishment he remained where we were sitting. I threw myself down*

*somehow under a certain figtree, and let my tears flow freely. Rivers
streamed from my eyes, a sacrifice acceptable to you (Ps. 50:19),
and (though not in these words, yet in this sense) I repeatedly said
to you: "How long, O Lord? How long, Lord, will you be angry to
the uttermost? Do not be mindful of our old iniquities." (Ps. 6:4).
For I felt my past to have a grip on me. It uttered wretched cries:
"How long, how long is it to be?" "Tomorrow, tomorrow." "Why not
now? Why not an end to my impure life in this very hour?"*

29

*As I was saying this and weeping in the bitter agony of my heart,
suddenly I heard a voice from the nearby house chanting as if it
might be a boy or a girl (I do not know which), saying and repeat-
ing over and over again "Pick up and read, pick up and read." At
once my countenance changed, and I began to think intently
whether there might be some sort of children's game in which such
a chant is used. But I could not remember having heard of one. I
checked the flood of tears and stood up. I interpreted it solely as a
divine command to me to open the book and read the first chapter I
might find. For I had heard how Antony happened to be present at
the gospel reading, and took it as an admonition addressed to himself when the words were read: "Go, sell all you have, give to the
poor, and you shall have treasure in heaven; and come, follow me"
(Matt. 19:21). By such an inspired utterance he was immediately
"converted to you" (Ps. 50:15). So I hurried back to the place
where Alypius was sitting. There I had put down the book of the
apostle when I got up. I seized it, opened it and in silence read the
first passage on which my eyes lit: "Not in riots and drunken par-
ties, not in eroticism and indecencies, not in strife and rivalry, but
put on the Lord Jesus Christ and make no provision for the flesh in
its lusts" (Rom. 13:13-14).*

*I neither wished nor needed to read further. At once, with the
last words of this sentence, it was as if a light of relief from all
anxiety flooded into my heart. All the shadows of doubt were dis-
pelled.*[1]

Note

1. Saint Augustine, *Confessions*, trans. Henry Chadwick (New York: Oxford
   University Press, 1992), pp. 152-153.

Using a Journal to Realize Your Future

CROSSROADS & PATTERNS

The future has great power over us. When it is filled with dread, we retreat into the past, but when it is filled with hope, we stride forward.

Group Note:
Leader's Notes for this session can be found on page 110.

I once had a colleague who taught a course on "The History of the Future." Of course, you can't discuss the "history" of something that has not yet happened. So the way he taught the course was to look at current trends and speculate where they were leading. This is how we can approach our future: by understanding our past and noticing the trajectories that point into the future.

For example, when reflecting on your past, you remember that as a kid you were always building things: birdhouses, railroad villages, forts. In high school you got As in shop class. You went on to get a degree in civil engineering. Sometimes the trajectory in your life is clear.

But at other times trajectories are not so obvious. For example, as you scan the past periods of your life, you find that people are important in each period. In fact, different people define different periods for you. Furthermore, in each instance you are in a relationship where you are able to help the other person. In light of this, as you consider the ministry or career to which God is calling you, it makes sense to go into a helping profession of some kind. But you may miss this fact since "helping others" is just something you do. You hardly notice. You assume everybody is like this.

When we are clear about the direction in which God has been nudging us, we can make sensible decisions about training, about lay ministry, about how to structure our lives, about how to use our time, about where and how to live. For the follower of Christ, it is important to become what God wants us to become. We have a strong and curious sense that our lives are supposed to matter, that we have a part to play in the unfolding drama of God's kingdom, and that who we become is important. The challenge is to find the future God has for us. This is where journals can help.

When we have an idea of what God has done in the past, we are better able to make choices for the future. When we're given the option of going in various directions, a clear sense of how we've been shaped and gifted by God makes it easier to choose.

Session Overview
One way to discern God's future for you is to pay attention to the past. Your future is often hidden in your past. In this session you will learn two ways of journaling. In the first, the Crossroads exercise, you will discern new possibilities in your future by finding past roads you did not (or could not) follow at the time. These may be new roads that you can now walk along. In the second, the Patterns exercise, you will reflect on the past to discern who you have become and, ideally, to know where you should go. (Since there won't be time to practice both exercises with a group, you'll be learning the Patterns method during the coming week.)

TELLING OUR STORIES   15-20 Minutes
Some day . . .
Most of us dream about the future: what we will "someday" become, where we will go, what we will do. These dreams are almost always bright and wonderful.

1. When you were a child, what did you dream of becoming?

   ❑ a professional (doctor, lawyer, dentist, minister, accountant)
   ❑ a service worker (firefighter, police officer, ambulance driver)
   ❑ a business person (CEO, accountant, boss, salesperson)
   ❑ a wanderer (scuba instructor, beach bum, explorer)
   ❑ a parent
   ❑ an athlete
   ❑ an entertainer
   ❑ a recluse
   ❑ a teacher
   ❑ other:

2. By your senior year in high school, how had your plans changed? Why?

3. a. Which of your life dreams, if any, have you realized?

   b. Which do you hope to realize in the future?

   c. What new dreams do you now have?

JOURNALING METHOD   5 Minutes

Crossroads

We are forced to make choices. Contrary to the ad, it's not possible to "have it all." Some choices are small and of little consequence: to order fish or chicken at a restaurant; to pick an action video or a comedy. Other choices carry major consequences: to go to college or to start work; to take drugs or to stay clean. The big choices—the Crossroads choices—move us in new and decisive directions.

For example, Janet was just finishing junior college and wanted to go to art school. In her two years of college, it had become clear to her what she loved to do. It also had become clear that she wanted to spend the rest of her life with Pete, and he wanted to marry her. Janet was at a crossroads. She could get married or she could go to art school. She could not do both; there was not enough money. So Janet chose to get married. She would delay art school eighteen months until Pete finished his degree. But Janet got pregnant in their first year of marriage, so art school was put on hold.

We make a number of choices like the one Janet made. Sometimes we realize the magnitude or the implications of what we've chosen. Most of the time, we forget about the option we didn't choose.

But there may come a time when we can go back to a crossroads and start down the road we didn't take. At the time, that road was closed to us. But now the time has come to go in that direction.

This is one way to assess where to go in the future: by remembering crossroads from the past and discerning whether it is now time to explore the path not chosen.[1]

Janet is now forty-two years old and the mother of three. The children are older and independent. Pete is a high school principal. Janet feels that the time has finally come to take the other road. She will earn her art degree.

Patterns

There is a second way of working with the past in order to gain a sense of the future. In this exercise, scan what you've written about the various periods in your life, looking for the following:

- ❖ *Skills:* What are you good at? What have you been trained in?
- ❖ *Service:* What forms of service have you tried? Enjoyed? Desire to participate in?
- ❖ *Success:* Where have you found success in your life?
- ❖ *Failure:* Where have you been less than successful? (It is good to know what not to pursue.)
- ❖ *Joy:* What brings you joy in life?
- ❖ *Longings:* What have you always wanted to do?

As you explore each of these areas, you will develop a deeper appreciation of the patterns in your life. Thus you will have a better sense of where you can go in the future.

JOURNALING EXERCISE   15-30 Minutes

Preparation

There are three parts to this exercise: *Identifying a Crossroads, Exploring the Road Not Taken*, and *Considering Your Life Direction.*

To begin, first take out your journal and find a comfortable spot for writing. Date your entry, and entitle it "Crossroads." (If you are organizing your journal into categories, file this exercise in the History section.)

Next, do the focusing exercise on page 107. (If you are meeting with a group, the leader will guide you in this process.) Your aim at this point is to relax, focus on the topic, and ask the Holy Spirit to lead you as you journal.

Identifying a Crossroads

Identify a Crossroads event: Go back to a particular period in your life and look for crossroads. Scan your reflections on different periods until you find such an event. Once you have identified the event you wish to explore, write up to three paragraphs describing the Crossroads as clearly as you can.

Exploring the Road Not Taken

Explore the road not taken by using your imagination: Picture yourself back at the place where you made the choice, but this time choose to go in the other direction. Imagine what would have happened. Watch your life unfold as you walk this new road. Write down your imaginary journey in your journal.

Considering Your Life Direction

Recalling past crossroads is not the same as choosing to walk an untraveled road. In fact, most of the time the other road is still closed to us. We've lost interest. We have become different people. Or the option is no longer available to us. But sometimes we come upon a road we still need to walk. What we need to know is whether this is the time to do it and if this is God's will. Reflect on the following questions:

❖ Why does this road still hold interest for you?
❖ What price would you have to pay to walk it?

❖ What good would come from walking it?
❖ Does this road violate your integrity, commitments, or obedience to God's moral or ethical guidelines?
❖ How would this affect your life, especially your relationships?
❖ What is your sense when you pray about this?

Option: you may be at a Crossroads now. Instead of doing the above exercise, use the exercise below to explore your options:

❖ Describe your options as clearly as possible.

❖ In your mind, imagine yourself as you walk down one of the roads. What might this future look like? Now go back in your imagination to the other option, and consider what life would be like if you chose it.

❖ Review your journal accounts of walking down each road. What new insights do you gain?

JOURNAL SHARING   **20-30 Minutes**

When you finish journaling, discuss your findings with the group, record them in your journal, or discuss them with a close friend.

1. Explore the process of journaling:

    a. What was the easiest part of the process for you? Why?

    b. What was the most difficult part of the process for you? Why?

    c. What new thing did you learn about how to journal?

2. Share your insights from the journal experience:

    a. What Crossroads event did you investigate? Was it easy or hard to find this event? Why were you drawn to it?

    b. What happened when you explored the road you didn't take?

    c. Is this untraveled road still interesting to you? If so, is it an appropriate path to explore based on the criteria listed on pages 58-59?

    d. Is now the time to travel it? If not now, when?

    e. How did you answer the questions in the "Considering Your Life Direction" portion of the exercise (pages 58-59)?

3. Pray about this experience:

    a. Ask God to guide you as you reflect on the future, to protect you from running off in the wrong direction, and to reveal the right one to you. Pray that you will be able to wisely apply what you learn.

    b. What would you like the group to pray about for you?

JOURNALING ASSIGNMENT

During the coming week, read over all of the material in the session, including the following excerpt from *Markings* by Dag Hammarskjöld.

Work on the issue of untraveled roads. Explore other time periods with this question in mind. Investigate different roads that appear to have some potential for you right now. Do the Patterns exercise (pages 56-57).

As at the end of the Journaling Exercise, ask God to guide you as you reflect on the future, to protect you from running off in the wrong direction, and to reveal the right direction to you. Pray that you will be able to apply what you learn.

Discern new insights you have into your unfolding story. What new things have you learned about the shape and character of your spiritual pilgrimage by examining these untraveled roads?

Decide what you want to share with the group during the next session from your Crossroads exercise.

JOURNAL READING

Dag Hammarskjöld, who was secretary general of the United Nations at the time of his death, considered his diary as a sort of 'White Book' concerning his negotiations with himself—and with God. The diary is curious in that it contains no references to his work as a diplomat, no comment on the famous people he met nor on the historical events he participated in. Rather, it is the story of his slow movement from despair to faith in God. W. H. Auden, who worked on the translation of *Markings*, commented that in reading it one has the privilege of being in contact with a great, good, and lovable man.

4.8.59
To have humility is to experience reality, not in relation to ourselves, but in its sacred independence. It is to see, judge, and act from the point of rest in ourselves. Then, how much disappears, and all that remains falls into place.

In the point of rest at the centre of our being, we encounter a world where all things are at rest in the same way. Then a tree becomes a mystery, a cloud, a revelation, each man a cosmos of whose riches we can only catch glimpses. The life of simplicity is simple, but it opens to us a book in which we never get beyond the first syllable.

Easter, 1960
Forgiveness breaks the chain of causality because he who "forgives" you—out of love—takes upon himself the consequences of what you have done. Forgiveness, therefore, always entails a sacrifice.

The price you must pay for your own liberation through another's sacrifice is that you in turn must be willing to liberate in the same way, irrespective of the consequences to yourself.

Whitsunday, 1961
I don't know Who—or what—put the question, I don't know when it was put. I don't even remember answering. But at some moment I did answer Yes to Someone—or Something—and from that hour I was certain that existence is meaningful and that, therefore, my life, in self-surrender, had a goal.

From that moment I have known what it means "not to look back" and "to take no thought for the morrow."

Led by the Ariadne's thread of my answer through the labyrinth of Life, I came to a time and place where I realized that the Way leads to a triumph which is a catastrophe, and to a catastrophe which is a triumph, that the price for committing one's life would be reproach, and that the only elevation possible to man lies in the depths of humiliation. After that, the word "courage" lost its meaning since nothing could be taken from me.

As I continued along the Way, I learned, step by step, word by word, that behind every saying in the Gospels, stands one man and one man's experience. Also behind the prayer that the cup might pass from him and his promise to drink it. Also behind each of the words from the Cross.[2]

Notes
1. This is how Dr. Ira Progoff describes this exercise.
2. Dag Hammarskjöld, *Markings*, translated by Leif Sjöberg and W. H. Auden (London: Faber and Faber, 1964).

SESSION SIX

Using a Journal
to Explore Your
Emotional Responses

CREATIVITY & DREAMS

*So murky, so hidden, yet so potent.
To know myself from within . . . so
powerful, so difficult, so vital.*

Group Note:
Leader's Notes for
this session can be
found on page 111.

To speak of an inner world is to recognize
that who we are is not just what we do.
We are what we feel, what we dream,
what we imagine, what we long for, what
we hear God saying to us—all of this is a
vital part of who we are. Journals are a powerful tool for exploring this inner world.

Take feelings—we all feel. We differ, however, in our ability
to identify and express our feelings. Men, in particular, often
have a difficult time experiencing the emotional side of life. It is
important to explore our emotions, and journals allow us to do
this: to identify our feelings and then to express them in appropriate ways.

First, it's important to identify in our journals what we're
feeling, rather than let vague emotions swirl around inside us.
Ignoring or suppressing our feelings is not a healthy practice.
The second step is to learn how to express those emotions, especially the negative ones. Sometimes it's enough simply to write
down what we're feeling, or to write a letter that we will never
send. At other times, however, we'll need to express our feelings
directly to the people concerned. Journaling allows us to think

63

through how we deal with our emotions.

And what about our dreams? Everybody dreams, though we differ in our ability to remember them. Dreams are often a clue to what is going on in our inner lives. They "express the outward circumstances of a person's life, his current problems and fears, and also the hopes and goals toward which he is consciously planning. In addition, however, dreams reflect the deeper-than-conscious goals that are trying to unfold in a person's life," according to Dr. Ira Progoff. He has pointed out that dreams also bring to the fore destructive patterns and purposes in a person's life, of which he or she is unaware.[1]

God can speak to us also through dreams. This is certainly the case in the Bible. For example, Jesus' own life was preserved by Joseph's willingness to pay attention to his dreams (Matthew 2:19-23).

Along with our dreams, there are all of those images, reflections, thoughts, and intuitions that make up the substance of our inner world. We can learn a lot about ourselves by bringing these things to the surface, identifying them, and writing them down. Then we can own our inner world, deal with it, accept or reject it, process it, and pray about it.

Session Overview

A journal is a useful tool for getting in touch with the many dimensions of the inner life: feelings, dreams, reflections, intuitions, creativity, and the sense of God's presence.

Two ways of journaling are suggested in this session. In the first, the Creativity exercise, we try a simple method to evoke a creative response. In the second, the Dreams exercise, we work with our dream record to find insights that will be useful in our growth.

TELLING OUR STORIES   15-20 Minutes

The call to create . . .
Everyone is creative. Our creativity is a human-sized echo of God's.

1. When you were a child, in what way(s) did you express your creativity?

   ❏ with my hands
   ❏ through my mind
   ❏ through what I said
   ❏ in my play
   ❏ through my singing
   ❏ in my relationships
   ❏ other:

2. Which creative outlet(s) do you like most? Which do you long to do? Which area is unexplored?

   ❏ painting   ❏ dance
   ❏ drawing   ❏ relationships
   ❏ storytelling   ❏ decorating
   ❏ music   ❏ media
   ❏ cooking   ❏ sewing
   ❏ child rearing   ❏ wood/metalworking
   ❏ crafts   ❏ journaling
   ❏ poetry   ❏ video
   ❏ sculpture   ❏ composing
   ❏ writing   ❏ designing
   ❏ other:

3. What have you created that has given you the most satisfaction?

JOURNALING METHOD   **5 Minutes**

Creativity

You are a creative person. You can't help it—you are made in God's image, and God is by nature a creative being. The problem is that we don't always recognize our creativity. Your journal is a vehicle through which to discover and explore your creativity.

Creativity can be revealed in a variety of ways. Part of the challenge is to discover the medium that best expresses your creative spirit—pottery, poetry, writing, or painting, for example. Don't be deterred by the thought that you need to master a technique. Just begin. No one else will see your journal. Pick the creative outlet that appeals to you most. Be playful, and don't put any pressure on yourself to "be creative."

If words appeal to you, play with them. Write a poem, reconstruct a conversation, articulate an important thought, or write a letter. Put words to paper. See where this leads. Don't critique what you produce. Editing and reworking will come later.

If images and shapes appeal to you, start sketching. Draw a face, copy a design, doodle, sketch a cartoon. Or simply let lines flow from your pen. See what happens.

Maybe you like numbers. So did Einstein—a very creative guy. What interests you about numbers? What draws you to them? Play around with them, or the idea of them, and see what you come up with. You can do the same thing with musical patterns.

Another aspect of creativity is content. It's not merely how you express yourself, but what you express. What really matters to you? What do you have to say? Why? To whom? Wrestle with what matters to you. The combination of form and content is what creativity is all about.

Dealing with Dreams

The first step in dealing with dreams is to remember them. If recalling dreams is difficult for you, then you need to make plans before you go to sleep. This will involve several steps: First, tell yourself as you go to sleep, "I want to remember my dreams." Remind yourself several times. Second, put a pen and some paper beside your bed so that when you wake up, you can immediately jot down whatever dream you recall. Third, you even can set your alarm clock twenty minutes earlier than normal. This usually ensures that you will wake up in the middle of a dream.

The next step is exploring your dreams. It's best if you work with a series of dreams that you have recorded over time in your journal. Don't worry about interpreting them; simply make note of what you remember. As you read over the record of your dreams, be alert to impressions and insights. Are there recurring images? Do meanings jump out at you? What do the dreams make you feel? What connections do you sense between the dreams and your waking life? In other words, use dreams as clues to help you understand your inner life.[2]

By the way. . .

Although two journaling methods are described in this session, you will have time to work with only one of them initially. The other can wait until your journaling time during the coming week.

JOURNALING EXERCISE   15-30 Minutes
Preparation
There are two options to choose from this time: the Creativity exercise and the Dreams exercise.

To begin, take out your journal and find a comfortable spot for writing. Date your entry, and entitle it "Creativity" or "Dreams," depending on which exercise you have selected. (If you are organizing your journal into categories, file this exercise in either Musings or Dreams, depending on your choice.)

Next, do the focusing exercise on page 107. (If you are meeting with a group, the leader will guide you in this process.) Your aim at this point is to relax, focus on the topic, and ask the Holy Spirit to lead you as you journal.

Option 1: Creativity Exercise
Read Psalm 23. Do this slowly, two or three times, until you begin to get a sense for what is being said. When you feel ready, express Psalm 23 in a different format (select one of the following):

❖ Paraphrase it from your present situation or from the viewpoint of a person who is dying.

❖ Do a sketch (abstract or realistic) that captures the sense of the psalm.

❖ Write a poem about it.

❖ Have a conversation with the Lord.

❖ Outline a short story based on this psalm.

❖ Express it in music: write lyrics or the music; explain how you would express it if you were writing a symphony.

❖ Create a collage: paste together clippings from magazines that capture the sense of the psalm.

❖ Respond in your own creative way to the psalm.

After you complete the exercise, describe in your journal what the creative process was like for you.

Option 2: Dreams Exercise
In order to do this exercise, you need to have at least one

dream in your dream log that you can work with, though it is better if you have a series of dreams.

Review the dreams—slowly, thoughtfully, prayerfully. Record your impressions, thoughts, and questions as you do so.

Give the dream or dream sequence a title (what the dream is all about). Describe the central themes. Next, describe the emotional tone of the dreams. Finally, identify any questions that have been raised for you.[3]

After comparing your dream log with your work in the Daily Log and History entries, identify any links you see. In what ways does your inner life relate to your external life?

JOURNAL SHARING   **20-30 Minutes**

When you finish journaling, discuss your findings with the group, record them in your journal, or discuss them with a close friend.

1. Explore the process of journaling:

    a. What was the easiest part of the process for you? Why?

    b. What was the most difficult part of the process for you? Why?

    c. What new thing did you learn about how to journal?

2. Share your insights from the journal experience:

    a. Which exercise did you do: the Creativity or the Dreams exercise? Why did you select it?

    b. For those who did the Creativity exercise: Which creative outlet did you choose to explore? Why? Talk about the results. What did you learn about creativity? About your potential as a creative person?

    c. For those who did the Dreams exercise: How many dreams did you consider? Talk about your dreams and the insights you gathered from them. What did you learn about the use of dreams in exploring your inner life?

    d. What new aspects of your story have you uncovered?

3. Pray about this experience. What single thing would you like to pray about, or have the group pray about for you?

JOURNALING ASSIGNMENT

During the next week spend some time reading through all the material in this session, including the excerpt from Evelyn Underhill's journal.

Explore your creativity. Identify past experiences of creativity. Try new and inventive responses to Scripture (or to incidents in your life that you want to express). Ask God to help you develop your creativity.

Explore your dream life. If you have not recorded any (or many) dreams, try to do so in the week ahead. Use the dreams you remember with the Dream exercise described on pages 68-69.

Discern new insights you have into your unfolding story. What new things have you learned about who you are?

Finally, decide what you want to share with your group during the next session from these exercises. You might want to share a creative piece with the group, but remember that you will have only a few minutes.

JOURNAL READING

Not all journals are written in notebooks and hidden away. Some journal entries come in the form of letters we send to trusted others. This was the case with the following excerpts from the life of Evelyn Underhill. In June 1923, she wrote about the steps in her spiritual pilgrimage to Baron Friedrich von Hügel.

Evelyn Underhill was a scholar and prolific early twentieth century British spiritual and theological writer. She was the first woman to lecture on theology at Oxford and the first woman to become a leader in retreat work in the Anglican community. Her classic works, *Mysticism* (1911) and *Worship* (1936), are still read today. She was also in great demand as a spiritual counselor. Upon her death *The Times* declared that she was the "spiritual director to her generation."

General
I feel quite different from last year: but in ways rather difficult to define. Deeper in. More steady on my knees though not yet very

steady on my feet. Not so rushing up and down between blankness and vehement consolations. Still much oscillation, but a kind of steady line persists instead of zigzags.

I have been trying all the time to shift the focus from feeling to will, but have not yet fully done it, and shall not feel safe till I have. The Christocentric side has become so much deeper and stronger—it nearly predominates. I never dreamed it was like this. It is just beginning to dawn on me what the Sacramental life really does involve: but it is only in flashes of miraculous penetration I can realize this. On the whole, in spite of blanks, times of wretched incapacity, and worse . . . I have never known such deep and real happiness, such a sense of at last having got my real permanent life, and being able to love without stint, where I am meant to love. It is as if one were suddenly liberated and able to expand all round. Such joy that it sometimes almost hurts. All this, humanly speaking, I owe entirely to you. Gratitude is a poor dry word for what I feel about it. I can't say anything.

Prayer
Prayer at good times though still mixed, is more Passive: a sort of inarticulate communion, or aspirations, often merely one word, over and over. Sometimes I wonder whether this is not too much taking the line of least resistance; but it is so wonderful, sweeps one along into a kind of warm inhabited darkness and blind joy— one lives in Eternity in that—can't keep at this pitch long, twenty minutes or so.

I do try to say a few psalms each day and do Intercessions, but one forgets everything then. Of course it's not always like this, often all distraction and difficulty.

Vocation
I feel great uncertainty as to what God chiefly wants of me. Selection has become inevitable. I can't meet more than half the demands made. I asked for more opportunity of personal service and have thoroughly been taken at my word! But there is almost no time or strength left now for study for its own sake; always giving or preparing addresses, advice, writing articles, trying to keep pace with work, going on committees and conferences—and with so little mental food I risk turning into a sort of fluid clergyman! More

serious, the conflict between family claims and duties and work is getting acute. *My parents are getting old: they don't understand, and are a bit jealous of the claims on my life (especially as it's all unpaid work). I feel perhaps I ought to have more leisure for them, though I do see them nearly every day. But this could only be done by reducing what seems like direct work for God, or my poor people or something. I confess the work and the poor people are congenial: and idling about chatting and being amiable, when there is so much to be done, a most difficult discipline—so I can't judge the situation fairly. It is not a case of being needed in any practical sense: just of one's presence being liked, and one's duties slightly resented![4]*

Notes

1. Progoff, p. 229.
2. If you want to pursue dream interpretation further, consult a book like *Dreams and Spiritual Growth: A Christian Approach to Dreamwork* by Louis M. Savary, Patricia H. Berne, and Stephon Kaplan Williams (New York: Paulist Press, 1984).
3. This is the TTAQ dreamwork technique found in Savary, Berne, and Williams, p. 22.
4. Margaret Cropper, *Evelyn Underhill* (London: Longmans, Green, and Co., 1958), pp. 105-110.

Using a Journal to Nurture Your Spiritual Life

LETTERS & PRAYER

To speak with God . . . how impossible. Yet, did not our fathers and mothers in the faith do so?

Group Note:
Leader's Notes for this session can be found on page 111.

Journaling is a spiritual discipline. A journal is a tool that enables us to remember, to probe, to understand, and to question our lives. In this way we grow spiritually. Journals are a wonderful tool for nurturing our spiritual lives because we can do so much in them. We can work at forming a God-centered worldview as we wrestle with ideas and learn to think theologically about life. In our journals we seek to understand ourselves better and to offer our lives up to God. In our journals we wrestle with the choices we face, seeking to know and do God's will. Most importantly, our journals provide a tool for discerning the presence of God in us, around us, and in other people.

Journaling also aids us in the practice of other spiritual disciplines.

Bible study: In our journals we take notes on a passage, record our observations, write down our questions, and reflect on the passage.

Prayer: In our journals we identify our requests, write out our prayers, copy other people's prayers as we learn to pray, and listen to what God is saying to us.[1]

Meditation: In our journals we reflect on our lives and actions in the context of our Bible study and prayer.

Confession: In our journals we tell God what we have done (which we ought not to have done) and what we have left undone (which we should have done).

Why are journals such a powerful force for spiritual change? There are several reasons. First, when we work in a journal, we put our thoughts, feelings, issues, and concerns into words on a page. The process of writing something down clarifies issues and keeps us honest. Second, journaling forces us to face ourselves and our unfolding lives. By working in a journal we are giving time to growth; we are actively working at it. Third, journals give us an ongoing record so that we know where we have come from, where we are, and where we are going. In knowing our past, we understand the present better and have a clearer reading of how to prepare for our future. Finally, journals enable us to know our stories. As we work in our journals, we piece together the various elements of our particular story. In understanding the nature of our pilgrimage, we come to know who God wants us to be and what we are called to do. We understand what "talents" we've been given and how to invest them. We discover questions to which we need answers. We see the choices we are called upon to make. In knowing our stories, we come to know God more personally. That is a great gift.

Session Overview
Communication with God is at the heart of our spiritual life: talking and listening to God. A journal is an aid to both of these processes. This session suggests two ways of journaling. In the first, the Letter to God exercise, we use our journals to express to God what we're thinking, feeling, and wrestling with. In the second, the Prayer exercise, we use our journals to learn new ways to pray.

TELLING OUR STORIES   **15-20 Minutes**

Experiencing God . . .

Experiences of God come in different ways to different people: sometimes they are big and dramatic; sometimes small and quiet. Most of the time, we hardly notice.

1. When you were a child, in what ways were you aware of God? Explain.

   ❏ in my prayers
   ❏ in the Bible
   ❏ in church
   ❏ in nature
   ❏ in certain experiences
   ❏ in reading
   ❏ in conversation
   ❏ other:

2. What's been the most direct experience you've had of God?

   ❏ a spine-tingling sense that God was present
   ❏ joyous, overwhelming worship
   ❏ a deep awareness of God's presence in nature
   ❏ a mystical experience
   ❏ an amazing answer to prayer
   ❏ my conversion experience
   ❏ nothing quite like any of this
   ❏ an inner sense of God's presence
   ❏ other:

3. What was your conversion experience like? Or what's the nearest thing you've had to a conversion experience?

JOURNALING METHOD   10 Minutes

Just as we have tried dialogue exercises with people and subjects (in session four), so we also can dialogue with God. The process is the same: write two to four paragraphs that define the state of your relationship to God. In a meditative manner, begin a dialogue with God and record the unfolding conversation in your journal. Once you are finished, review and respond to the dialogue.

For some people, this is a good way to understand their relationship with God. However, many people find it difficult to do this exercise. It feels presumptuous to write what we suppose God is saying. But the fact remains that we need to communicate with God. The following two exercises are alternate ways of doing the same thing: speaking to and listening to God.

A Letter to God

The process is simple: Write a letter to God. There is nothing more—or less—to the exercise. Here are some examples to give a perspective from which to write.

> *A note about everyday issues:* "Dear God, I'm sitting here worrying about Jerry again. He's a good kid, as you know, but he just can't get his act together. It's 11:00 A.M., and he still isn't home from the night he spent at Ben's house. So, another day of work is lost to partying. I'm so worried about him. . . ." In this way you define the issues that concern you and offer them to God.

> *A reflection on a period in your life:* "Dear God, I've spent the past few months working on my Kansas City phase of life. You know how troubled that time was. I'm really glad it's past. Help me never again to have to go through something like that. So now I offer that period to you. Here is what I've made of it. . . ." In this way you offer to God your reflections on your past and, in prayer, seek to learn from the past and leave it behind.

> *A meditation on an issue:* "Dear God, I don't understand why innocent children die. The tragedy in Algeria haunts me.

How could this happen? I know that you understand evil and death. You sent your own Son to suffer and die. . . ." In this way you examine your views on tough theological issues as you develop a Christian worldview.

A response to a challenge: "Dear God, I know it's good for me to live next door to the Smiths, but frankly, they drive me crazy with their loud music and loud friends. I know I'm supposed to love them, but I don't. Please help me with this. . . ." In this way you work your way through a problem of Christian discipleship.

Prayer

When we think of talking to God, we automatically think of prayer. But prayer isn't one thing, it's many. A journal is a good place to learn new ways to pray. You might want to experiment with the following three forms of prayer:

The Prayer of Examen: Saint Ignatius, the founder of the Jesuits, used this method. It's a way of assessing our day before God. It has three parts to it. You can use your journal to answer each of the following issues. During the past 24 hours:

1. Reflect on what you have to be *thankful* for. Let your prayer begin with joy and gratitude.

2. Reflect on the ways in which you have *met* God. Search through your day, pausing at the moments (mostly brief and incidental) in which you were aware that God's Spirit was present.

3. Reflect on the ways you have *avoided or failed* God. In this atmosphere of thankfulness and awareness of God, confess your sin and shortcoming, knowing that God forgives and heals.

The Prayer of Intercession: In this prayer, we ask God (as God invites us to do) for what we—and others—need in life. In your journal write down your requests, based on the three petitions in the Lord's Prayer:

1. *Give* us this day our daily bread: Jesus invites us to pray about matters of everyday living: food, clothing, illness, problems we face, relationships—all of the "mundane" issues of life can be brought to God.

2. *Forgive* us our debts: We bring our sins, burdens, hurts, shortcomings, pain in relationships—every aspect of our relationships can be brought to God.

3. *Deliver* us from evil: We offer to God the temptations we face, the desire for power, fame, money, acquisition, control—all of the many faces of evil can be brought to God.

The Prayer of Worship: This is a prayer of response: adoration of and thanks to God for all the wonders of life. We may need the help of others since it's possible that we won't always have the words to express what's in our hearts. You might want to purchase a book such as *The Oxford Book of Prayer*[2] and search its pages until you find prayers that best express what you want to say. Copy these prayers into your journal. Pray them often until their language becomes yours. Write down your own prayers of wonder and worship. Make your journal a place of rich prayer.[3]

JOURNALING EXERCISE   15-30 Minutes

Preparation

There are two options for today's exercise: Letter to God and
Prayer. Select whichever one you feel most interested in at this
time. You can explore the other during the coming week.

   To begin, take out your journal and find a comfortable spot
for writing. Date your entry, and entitle it "Letter to God" or
"Prayer," depending on which exercise you want to do. (If you
are organizing your journal into categories, file this exercise in
the Pilgrimage section.)

   Next, do the focusing exercise on page 107. (If you are
meeting with a group, the leader will guide you in this
process.) Your aim at this point is to relax, focus on the topic,
and ask the Holy Spirit to lead you as you journal.

Option 1: Letter to God

Follow the instructions on pages 78-79, and write a letter to
God. Instead of writing the letter, you may choose to do a dialogue with God, if you are comfortable with that. In either case,
speak with God about issues that are significant to you.

Option 2: Prayer

Select one of the prayer formats described on pages 79-80, and
use your journal to help you pray.

JOURNAL SHARING   **15-30 Minutes**

When you finish journaling, discuss your findings with the group, record them in your journal, or discuss them with a close friend.

1. Explore the process of journaling:

   a. What was the easiest part of the process for you? Why?

   b. What was the most difficult part of the process for you? Why?

   c. What new thing did you learn about how to journal?

2. Share your insights from the journal experience:

   b. Which exercise did you do: the Letter to God or the Prayer exercise? Why did you select the one that you did?

   b. For those who chose the Letter to God exercise: Read portions of your letter. What did you learn about your relationship to God from this exercise?

   c. For those who chose the Prayer exercise: Which prayer did you explore? Read your prayer or share insights from the experience. What did you learn about prayer?

   d. What new aspects of your story have you uncovered?

3. Pray about this experience. What single thing would you like to pray about, or have the group pray about for you?

JOURNALING ASSIGNMENT

At some point during the coming week, read over all the material in this chapter, including the following excerpt from *Pensées*, the journal of Blaise Pascal.

Next, explore your spiritual life. Identify experiences in which the life and presence of God was especially evident. Try new forms of prayer. Develop a new awareness of the spiritual side of your life.

Finally, ask God for help as you explore your spirituality. Discern new insights you have received into your unfolding story. What new things have you learned about who you are? Also, think about how you're going to continue to journal, now that this course is almost over.

JOURNAL READING

Blaise Pascal was a genius. At age eleven, he wrote a paper about sound in vibrating objects. At sixteen, his article on Conic Sections won the respect of mathematicians in Paris. As an adult, he constructed a machine to do arithmetic calculations. He also developed the barometer and defined the general laws of pneumatics. In addition to his scientific accomplishments, he was a man of letters. His book, *The Provincial Letters*, was a major influence in French literature. Pascal was also a devout Christian. Toward the end of his life (he died at thirty-nine) he started a book on evidences of religion. All he produced, however, were fragments. They were more like journal entries than book chapters. After his death, his friends published these as *Pensées*. The following excerpts show the use of a journal as a vehicle to clarify thoughts, to mull over ideas, and to develop theological understanding.

784:
I consider Jesus Christ in all persons and in ourselves: Jesus Christ as a Father in his Father, Jesus Christ as a Brother in his Brethren, Jesus Christ as poor in the poor, Jesus Christ as rich in the rich, Jesus Christ as Doctor and Priest in priests, Jesus Christ as Sovereign in princes, etc. For by his glory he is all that is great, being God; and by his mortal life he is all that is poor and abject.

Therefore he has taken this unhappy condition, so that he could be in all persons, and the model of all conditions.

785:
Jesus Christ is an obscurity (according to what the world calls obscurity), such that historians, writing only of important matters of states, have hardly noticed him.

791:
What man ever had more renown? The whole Jewish people foretell him before his coming. The Gentile people worship him after his coming. The two peoples, Gentile and Jewish, regard him as centre.

And yet what man enjoys this renown less? Of thirty-three years, he lives thirty without appearing. For three years he passes as an impostor; the priests and the chief people reject him; his friends and his nearest relatives despise him. Finally, he dies, betrayed by one of his own disciples, denied by another, and abandoned by all.

What part, then, has he in this renown? Never had man so much renown; never had man more ignominy. All that renown has served only for us, to render us capable of recognizing him; and he had none of it for himself.

796:
Proofs of Jesus Christ—Jesus Christ said great things so simply, that it seems as though he had not thought them great; and yet so clearly that we easily see what he thought of them. This clearness, joined to this simplicity, is wonderful.[4]

Notes
1. The process of reading the Bible reflectively is discussed in another volume in this series: *Contemplative Bible Reading: Experiencing God Through Scripture*. Methods of prayer are explored in *Meditative Prayer: Entering God's Presence*.
2. George Appleton, ed. (New York: Oxford University Press, 1985).
3. For more insight into the various forms of prayer, see Richard Foster, *Prayer: Finding the Heart's True Home* (New York: HarperCollins, 1992).
4. Blaise Pascal, *Pensées*, trans. W. F. Trotter (New York: Random House, 1941), pp. 275-279.

Using a Journal to Reflect on the Bible

BIBLE STUDY THROUGH NEW EYES

Is the Bible God's Journal?

Group Note:
Leader's Notes for this session can be found on page 111.

The Bible has always held a predominant place in Christian spirituality. Every tradition places it at the center of spiritual exploration. This is not surprising. Christians believe that Scripture is "God-breathed" (as the apostle Paul writes in 2 Timothy 3:16). By this Paul means that God was actively involved in the writing of Scripture so that what the Bible teaches is true and normative. No wonder Christians have explored Scripture with such diligence!

Journals assist us in this process of exploration.

Notekeeping: We can use a journal as a place to keep our notes as we puzzle over the meaning of a passage. We record insights gleaned from commentaries and Bible dictionaries. We jot down our own musings about the text. We write out the questions we have about the passage. This is journaling in aid of Bible study.

Application: Journals are of great use when it comes to applying Scripture to our lives. After all, this is the point of our exploration: not just to know what the Bible says (important as that is) but to be changed by what the Bible says. The process of contemplative Bible reading (or *lectio divina*, to use its Latin name) is a powerful way of letting the Bible speak to us.[1] Journals are the ideal place in which to note the words or phrases that speak to us, the connections between these words or phrases and our life, the prayers that we pray as a result of encountering a particular passage, and the impressions from God as we rest in a contemplative state with this passage in mind. This is journaling in aid of Bible application.

Creativity: Journals allow us to interact creatively with the Bible. We can use them to write out a paraphrase of the passage we studied. Or we can write a letter to a friend on the basis of what we learned from the Bible. We can draw a picture that captures the essence of the passage or write a poem (or music) that is inspired by the text. This is journaling in aid of the creative process.

Session Overview
In this chapter we will explore a new way to do Bible study based on a journaling perspective. The idea is simple. What do we see when we read through various incidents from one person's life? How can we retell that story in journal format? This will probably be a new way for you to study the Bible.

TELLING OUR STORIES   15-20 Minutes

Love and Marriage . . .

Since we'll be looking at the book of Ruth in this session, the following questions draw from the central issue of that book—finding a spouse. Though seeking a spouse is a deeply important part of life for many people—usually containing a mixture of excitement, trauma, wonder, agony, and fulfillment—there are also many who have not chosen that path. For those who are not married, please adapt these questions to your own circumstances.

1. Describe how you met the person who is (or was to become/might have become/you might like to become) your spouse.

2. What was the best part of your courtship (or courtship in general)? The worst part?

3. Which question would you like to ask the opposite sex about courtship? Let the opposite sex in your group reply!

JOURNALING METHOD   5 Minutes

Wouldn't it be wonderful if some of the folk we meet in the Bible had published journals? Then we could get in touch with not only what they did but how they felt. We would know the issues they wrestled with and how they nurtured their spiritual lives.

Alas, there are no existing journals of this sort from those ancient times. However, we do have accounts of various people in the Bible. Different vignettes drawn from their lives are recorded in the Bible. By reading over these accounts we can get a feel for these people and their experience with God. Then, by means of reflection, we can attempt to understand how they felt and what they were thinking in certain situations. We can, in other words, try to recreate their journal entries.

This is a different type of Bible study than most of us are used to. It begins with careful observation of what is written in the text. We also consider the background to the account. Then we ask: what do you suppose such a person thought and felt in that situation? This is a way to make connections between their lives and our lives. It is reading the text from a personal point of view. It is using imagination to understand ourselves better even as we come to understand better the people in the Bible. In this way we grow in our understanding of our own story as we reflect on the story of others.

JOURNALING EXERCISE   15-30 Minutes

Preparation

First take out your journal and find a comfortable spot for writing. Date your entry, and entitle it "The Journal of Ruth and Naomi." (If you are organizing your journal into categories, file this exercise in the Bible study section.)

Each person will select one of the following passages from the book of Ruth. Your goal is to respond in your journal to each of the three questions for that selection. The first question is designed to help you notice and understand what the passage is saying. The second question asks you to write what Ruth or Naomi might have written in her journal. The third question suggests one possible connection between their lives and your life. But you may see another connection which you wish to explore. The background notes will assist you in understanding your passage.

1. NAOMI AND RUTH: RUTH 1:1-14
   ❑ How had Naomi come to Moab in the first place and why did she decide to return to Bethlehem? On what basis does Naomi urge her daughters-in-law to remain in Moab?
   ❑ How might Naomi have described in her journal the period of time when she lived in Moab?
   ❑ What was the most difficult period in your life? Why? In what ways was the hand of God present during that difficult time?

2. RUTH COMES TO BETHLEHEM: RUTH 1:15-22
   ❑ Why does Ruth decide to accompany her mother-in-law into this foreign land?
   ❑ In her journal, how might Naomi have described how she felt when she returned to Bethlehem? What would she have written about Ruth?
   ❑ Is there anything in your life parallel to the experience of Ruth committing herself to Naomi and accompanying her on this journey into the unknown? Describe it and the outcome in your life.

3. RUTH MEETS BOAZ: RUTH 2:1-12
   ❑ Describe the circumstances under which Ruth and Boaz meet and how each responds. What does this passage teach about the character of Boaz? The character of Ruth?
   ❑ In her journal, what might Ruth have written about what it was like living in a foreign land as a widow with no income.
   ❑ Recall instances in which you have been unexpectedly blessed by the kindness of strangers, or in which you had what looked like a stroke of good luck? In what ways was God present in that experience?

4. RUTH REQUESTS MARRIAGE: RUTH 3:1-13
   ❑ In this rather unusual situation (to twentieth-century, Western eyes) what was the role of Naomi? The role of Ruth? The role of Boaz?
   ❑ How might Ruth have written about that night with Boaz?
   ❑ How did you come to be engaged (if you have been engaged)? How do we choose the person we intend spending our lives with?

5. BOAZ MARRIES RUTH: RUTH 4:1-12
   ❑ Describe how it comes to be that Boaz marries Ruth. How do you respond to these ancient ways of marriage?
   ❑ What might Ruth have written about her forthcoming marriage to Boaz?
   ❑ Describe your marriage (if you are married). How does it differ from Ruth's experience? In what ways was it similar?

6. RUTH BEARS A CHILD: RUTH 4:13-22
   ❑ What is the outcome of Naomi's story? Of Ruth's story? Of the story of Israel?
   ❑ How might Ruth have summed up her life in her journal?
   ❑ In what ways is your story intertwined with the stories of others? How have your actions impacted the story of your family?

Once you have identified the section you intend to examine in your journal, do the focusing exercise on page 107. (If you are meeting with a group, the leader will guide you in this process.) Your aim at this point is to relax, focus on the topic, and ask the Holy Spirit to lead you as you journal.

The Journal of Ruth and Naomi
Read over your selected passage several times. (If you have time, you may wish to quickly read through the rest of the book of Ruth—it is short.) Also glance at the following background notes, paying special attention to those that apply to your passage.

Once you have finished reading, work on the first question, jotting down your insights. Write out a journal entry as if you are Ruth or Naomi. Use your creative imagination (but stick to the outline of the passage).

As you journal, reflect on the connections between the life of these women and your own life. What do you learn from this connection that is valuable in your pilgrimage?

Background Notes

- ❖ *Moab:* A region on the east side of the Dead Sea. There was great hostility between those from Judah (one of the tribes of Israel located on the other side of the Dead Sea) and the Moabites. The source of this hostility was the Israelite invasion of the region. Bethlehem was on the west side of the Dead Sea, fifty miles or so from Moab.

- ❖ *Naomi's husband died:* It was almost impossible for a widow without sons to survive on her own. The social structure was such that when she lost her husband she lost her place in society and had to depend on others.

- ❖ *Ruth:* Ruth, who was a Moabitess not an Israelite, is the great-grandmother of King David and an ancestress of Jesus (see Matthew 1:1,5).

- ❖ *full/empty:* This is the key motif in this book. Naomi is stripped of everything but, due to the faithfulness of Ruth and the provision of God, she becomes full again.

- ❖ *harvest:* Grain was harvested in April and May. This involved the cutting of grain with a hand sickle, binding it into sheaves, threshing it (removing the grain from the stalk), and winnowing (tossing the grain into the air to separate the grain from the chaff).

- ❖ *leftover grain:* Old Testament law instructed farmers to leave behind the grain the harvesters missed and to allow the poor and the widowed to gather this for themselves.

- ❖ *Tonight he will be winnowing:* During harvest it was common for landowners to sleep near their grain so as to protect it from thieves.

- ❖ *Wash and perfume yourself:* These are the preparations a bride would make for her wedding day.

❖ *eating and drinking:* Harvest time was a time of celebration.

❖ *uncover his feet and lie down:* This whole situation in the threshing room strikes the modern reader as aggressive (on Naomi's part in her instructions to Ruth) and sexually charged. In fact, it was more innocent than it appears. Ruth's actions (guided by Naomi) were a request for marriage, appealing to Boaz in his role as the kinsman-redeemer. In this case, Boaz already had displayed his concern for and interest in Ruth so that Naomi is aware that he might find it attractive to marry her. In this whole situation Ruth's character is never in doubt (see 3:11).

❖ *kinsman-redeemer:* The closest male relative had the responsibility to marry a widow. Boaz must give the kinsman-redeemer the opportunity to marry Ruth if he chooses.

❖ *town gate:* This is where business was conducted in ancient villages. The town elders assembled here, and all sorts of transactions took place.

❖ *you acquire the dead man's widow:* In order to keep alive the name of Mahlon, Ruth's dead husband, her first-born son would bear his name and inherit the land. The unnamed kinsman fears (perhaps) that should he have a son by Ruth and this prove to be his only heir, all his land would go to the family of Elimelech (Naomi's dead husband), leaving his family without land.

JOURNAL SHARING   20-30 Minutes

The order of sharing is changed for this session. Begin with insights from the story of Ruth. If you are doing this exercise with a group, let the group that did the first section go first, then move to the second passage, and so on. In this way everyone will develop a feel for the whole book of Ruth.

Do not spend all your time on question 1 because you have important decisions to make in this final session of the small group series. And you will want to allow everyone time to summarize what they have learned about journaling.

1. Share your insights from this journal experience:

   a. What did you learn about Ruth and Naomi?
   b. What did you learn about studying the Bible?
   c. What was the most valuable insight from this exercise into yourself and your spiritual journey?

2. Explore the whole process of journaling:

   a. What aspects of this journaling exercise were the easiest for you? The most difficult? The most useful? Why?
   b. What is your plan for continuing journaling once the group ends?
   c. What was the most important thing you learned about how to journal during the eight sessions?

3. Discuss the next step for your small group. Now that this overview of journaling is ending, you may wish to embark on another course in this series, such as *Spiritual Autobiography*. Your journaling work is the ideal preparation for writing and then sharing a spiritual autobiography.

4. Pray together. Praise God for what you've learned about journaling as a spiritual discipline. Thank God for what you've learned about your spiritual pilgrimage.

JOURNALING ASSIGNMENT

In your journal, continue to explore the story of Ruth and
Naomi. Read through the whole book. Look at the other five
passages. Be attentive to the parallels between their stories and
your story. In your journal, reflect further on the incidents in
your life that you recalled during the small group discussion.
Be alert to a new understanding of your past as it emerges in
the light of Scripture.

JOURNAL READING

Jim Elliot was one of five young missionaries murdered by the
Auca Indians in Ecuador in 1956. His journal was later edited
(but not abridged) by his widow, Elisabeth Elliot. This is the
kind of journal most men and women write. It was never
intended to be published. It records the ordinary struggles and
victories of an honest and devout young man who sought to
know and serve God. This excerpt was written in Ecuador
sometime between 1952 and 1955.

Notice that Jim Elliot used his journal not only to reflect on
his life, but as a tool for creative reflection on the Bible.

June 8
Heard brother Crisman (fifty years in Ecuador) at the Second
Church in the morning. Lord, let me learn to speak Spanish in fifty
years—seems as if no one really gets past the beginner's stage in
pronunciation of all the gringos I've met. And none hit the
national's genius of language. Give of the gift of tongues! Let me
speak to them as they ought to be spoken to, so they do not have to
hide their real reaction with polite praise. Glad to be in a national
home—at least to hear it spoken as a living-thought medium—
not merely as English translation.

Mist and rain under the slim, sharp silhouetted eucalyptus
with her [his future wife, Betty], then the mud-arch doorway out
of the wet. Talked of her relation with Dorothy and some of the
problems. Lord, I'm asking for the very best for them; let them
learn friendship in the full sense. Betty doesn't seem to really want
intimacy with D. J.—something my personality will never under-
stand. Let me deal wisely here, Lord, if I should counsel or suggest.
Felt very much outside the situation as far as really being able to

*analyze it, yet somehow so close to it with my feelings for Betty—
wanting the very happiest for her, and sensing a certain responsibility to achieve it for her. She admits a problem and confesses that she
doesn't know the way through it, but I fear she doesn't really want
it solved badly enough. Her natural reserve is strong; she only gets
intimate with those who "happen to fit"—or, as she says, "with
those friendships that are outright gifts from God." Although she
recognizes that some friendships must be made, I think she is not
willing to expend the effort to make one with D. J.—mainly because
she doesn't believe that they are a pair, she doesn't think D. will
really be capable of being "made" a comrade.*

*I agree. D. doesn't look like the right kind of stuff. But, oh, how
I want to see Betty happy these waiting years without each other,
and an intimate with whom she could share things would be such a
boon. Still, she says as I said when D. was en route to New York,
they have nothing in common. Outwardly, no. Betty is poetic, fond
of nature, penetrating. Dorothy seems superficial, childish, ingenu-
ous beside her. But, Father, they have Christ in common, and I
want you to teach them how to share him. I can't expect D. to be
for Betty what Pete has been for me, but at least she can be some
sort of outlet to confer with, some sort of balance to stabilize all
Betty's inwardness. Sure seems like a good problem, Lord. I am
waiting to see you work it out.*

October 6/2 Corinthians 1
*Second Corinthians 1 was my morning meditation. Stirred to sober
wonder at what, or rather who, shall be my glorying in the day of
Jesus Christ? O Lord, how little deliverance I have wrought in the
earth when compared with all Thy lavish promises of fruit. God
grant me effectiveness in life and balance. Also read some
Nietzsche this afternoon. He uses constantly the idea of "something
over there"—the man beyond—the "ubermensch." Dreadful con-
trast he makes with my Heavenly Prophet, but he points up, not in
the same direction.*[2]

Notes
1. This is the topic of *Contemplative Bible Reading: Experiencing God Through
   Scripture*, another volume in the Spiritual Disciplines Series.
2. Jim Elliot, *The Journals of Jim Elliot*, ed. Elisabeth Elliot (Old Tappan, NJ:
   Revell, 1978), pp. 393-394.

THE ART OF JOURNALING

We each have a story. Our stories tell who we are as they chart the unfolding of our lives, the things that make us unique. Journaling helps us make sense of our stories, understand their significance, and connect them with God's story.

Journals are a tool for reflection. There is great power in putting thoughts on a page. The very act of writing down an idea often sparks additional thoughts, insights, and concerns. You begin with a wisp of a thought and before you know it, you're on to something important in your life.

Anyone who has chosen to follow Christ has a very definite and specific goal in life—to become conformed to the image of Jesus Christ—and journaling can help us attain that goal. To be like Jesus is to become all we long to be and all we are meant to be. But to attain such a goal we need to know ourselves as well. Only by comparing who we are to who Jesus is can we discern the nature of the gap between the real and the ideal. It is by understanding this gap that we recognize those areas of our lives that need change.

Journaling can serve as a vehicle for exploration of who we have been, who we are now, and who we hope to become. Ultimately, spiritual formation is about growing in conformity to the image of Christ. While we can never *fully* attain to such a goal—there will always be a gap—it is crucial to aim towards it, for the goal of becoming like Jesus draws us into the future.

This course shows you how journaling can assist your spiritual growth. Its focus is on three areas:

❖ How to construct a journal
❖ How to use a journal to discern your personal story
❖ How to use a journal to trace your spiritual development

You can use this guide with a group of friends or on your own. Using it with a group will help a great deal, as you will see if you review some of the group exercises. But if you don't have anyone handy, don't let that stop you. However, if you show this guide to a few friends, you may discover a group has been there all along, waiting to be formed.

Constructing a Journal

A journal is simple: blank pages in a notebook or a folder on your hard drive. However, there are ways to construct a journal that make it a better tool for growth. The following instructions about binding, size, and paper assume you are writing by hand in a notebook, rather than on a computer. Of course, if you do the exercises in this guide with a group, you will probably be journaling with pen and paper during group time. Many people prefer the connection between self and paper that handwriting gives. Others prefer to journal on a computer, so a few suggestions for computer journaling are included as well.

Binding: While you can purchase bound books of blank pages with colorful covers, for this course you might prefer a journal that uses dividers (for organization of your writing). Also, you may find that loose-leaf binders give you more freedom to record "ordinary" and "mundane" thoughts. Bound volumes sometimes have an air of sanctity about them, which makes you feel that you must write carefully, spell accurately, and record only profound thoughts. Whatever binding you choose, be sure it is physically comfortable for you to write in; if the binding hurts your hand, it will distract you from writing.

Dividers: A journal is not just a diary in which you record each day's impressions. In a journal you record a variety of impressions, written from different vantage points and in different ways, with one section feeding into other sections. Thus, to maximize the value of the journal, it helps to divide it into sections. The following divisions are suggested:

- ❖ *Daily:* staying in touch with your life as it unfolds
- ❖ *History:* reconstructing the contours of your past
- ❖ *Dialogue:* journaling a "conversation"
- ❖ *Pilgrimage:* exercises to promote personal growth
- ❖ *Bible study:* analyzing and applying Scripture
- ❖ *Dreams:* recording your nightly images
- ❖ *Musings:* recording insights, thoughts, and reflections
- ❖ *Family:* marking key events in your family's development
- ❖ *Work:* keeping notes and materials related to your job

Size: There is no single or proper size for a journal. Larger formats permit more flexibility of use; smaller sizes are easier to carry. You can decide what size fits your life habits. You may have to experiment a little to find the size that is most comfortable and convenient for you.

Paper: Whether you use lined or unlined paper is also a personal choice. I find that I need lines to guide my writing. Others prefer blank pages, especially if they do a lot of sketching. Of course, you can use both!

Journaling on a computer: These days, some people think nothing of bringing a laptop to a group meeting, and a computer provides flexible filing. If you prefer to journal on a computer, create a folder called "Journal." Within that folder, create nine folders called "Daily," "History," "Dialogue," "Pilgrimage," "Bible study," "Dreams," "Musings," "Family," and "Work." Each time you add an entry to one of the folders, its filename should begin with a date designation so that the entries will appear in your menu in chronological order. You can achieve chronological order by designating the date in digits as year-month-day. For example:

> 990711.doc.................entry for July 11, 1999
> 001103 jill's bd...........thoughts on Jill's birthday; 11/3/00

Obviously, entries after December 31, 1999, will precede those before that date, but that's unimportant in a journal. (If the millennium problem bothers you and your system permits a longer filename, you can always use 19990711 and 20001103!)

Using a Journal
The mechanics of journaling are important. Once in place, they provide the right context in which to do serious work. It is important to reflect on these issues and make choices.

When should I journal? The short answer is "regularly." Just what "regularly" means will vary from person to person. Few people are able to journal on a daily basis—at least not for weeks or months at a time. The point is: use your journal to assist you; do not let it become a burden. However, when you are learning, try to journal at least three times a week for a while until the process becomes natural and easy for you.

As to time of day, this also will vary from person to person. Some people need the freshness of morning when the mind is clear. Others will journal at the end of the day as a way to process the day's experiences. Still others journal at a point during their day when they have some quiet time. If you have no idea what time of day is best for you, experiment! Schedule the same time of day for three days of your first week. (If you are a busy person, write into your calendar: "12:30-1:00, journaling.") If that time of day doesn't work out, choose a different time for the next week.

Where should I journal? You need a place where you can be alone and undisturbed. Journaling requires silence. You need inner space to reflect, pray, write, and read. Distractions make that difficult. Beyond this, people's needs vary. Find a setting that is comfortable and relaxing for you.

How long should I journal? If possible, you should journal for as long as it takes to process what you are working with. In practice, people have limited time and must make do with whatever time is available. When you are learning to journal, try to set aside half-hour blocks of time in order to get a feel for each journal exercise.

How should I journal? Date each entry, including the year. Give a title to the entry so you will know where to file it. Then start writing. Don't worry about spelling, grammar, or complete sentences; just make it legible enough so that you can go back and read it at a later date.

Privacy is important because total honesty is essential. Unless you are confident that you are writing for your eyes only, you won't be completely candid. A journal is where you can express yourself without reservation or fear of consequences. While you may decide later to share portions of your journal with others, don't write with that thought in mind, or you might tailor what you write for their eyes. If you journal on your computer, be sure to have some sort of security system that will allow only you to access the files.

What should I write? The various exercises in this book will guide you in what to write. Your attitude is important as you work on the exercises. An attitude of faith, of playfulness, of hope—and a willingness to acknowledge the way things really are—will increase the value of journaling in your life.

 Begin the process of journaling with prayer. Ask the Holy Spirit, whose role is to help us see God, to guide you and guard you as you probe inner issues. Then trust God. This is the difference between a journal and a spiritual journal: conscious trust in God and dependence upon God's leading as you write.

Using a Journal to Discern Your Story

Journals are the first step in preparing a *spiritual autobiography*. Through journal reflection, we get in touch with our past, recognize what is happening to us in the present, and develop a sense of where our future lies. As we do this, we begin to recognize the hand of God at work in our lives. The pieces of our past merge and become parts of a divine mosaic. A spiritual autobiography, then, is the selection of incidents from a life that reveals the spiritual thread that wends its way through that life.[1]

Using a Journal to Grow Spiritually

Journaling is itself a spiritual discipline. It focuses mind and heart on the issues of growth with the aim of discerning what God is doing in one's life. By using a journal, we come in touch with our cutting edges of growth, those areas where questions exist or where there is need or longing. These are the areas in which the Holy Spirit often seems most active.

Journaling is also an aid to other spiritual disciplines. Writing down your insights is helpful in Bible study. Writing out your prayers helps you to communicate with God. Creating a poem that praises God is an act of worship. Journaling with others and sharing your work can create a spiritual community.

The Power of Journaling in Groups

We need others as we learn the spiritual disciplines. For example, it is hard to pray regularly and consistently on our own. Worshiping God occurs in a corporate (as well as a private) setting. We need the insights of others as we study Scripture. Likewise, many people will learn to journal—and will be motivated to journal—by meeting with others who also are involved in this task.

Groups assist both the beginner and the experienced journaler. For the beginner, the rudiments of journaling are clarified as group members share how they experience the process. For the experienced journaler, a group will push him or her in new directions.

The journaling techniques you learn in each session will define the journaling process. At first, a new activity may feel somewhat strange. Keep working at it until it is comfortable and familiar to you. Eventually, you'll discover that some journal exercises work better for you than others. That's fine. There's nothing sacred about any particular exercise. They are simply tools designed to help you understand the meaning of your story.

A small group provides you the opportunity to share what you have learned about your pilgrimage with others who are also engaged in a spiritual pilgrimage. This is important because *journaling is never an end in itself; it is a means to spiritual growth.*

Triggers

Writing in each section of your journal is not always a straightforward process. For example, you may begin at a place in your past, trying to get a feel for a troubling incident. You write down the key people in your life at that time, and your sister's name triggers a thought of something you were supposed to do. The memory is troubling, beyond just the feeling of guilt over not keeping a commitment. So you shift over to the Present Period log and work there for a while as you try to make sense of what is going on inside you. (you will learn more about this in session one.)

Pay attention to triggers—those thoughts that spark memories, feelings, or ideas that sneak into your consciousness.

These are not the issues you began reflecting on; almost without warning, your mind moves to a new place. Be willing to give these "tangents" some space; they may prove to be quite important.

Or the tangent may just be that—a tangent. For example, it is not uncommon for a person to begin to pray, only to be reminded of a whole host of things he must do. This is a diversion from your real task. Over time, you will learn which tracks to follow and which to set aside so you can get back to the real issue.

Note

1. Another book in this series, *Spiritual Autobiography: Discovering and Sharing Your Spiritual Story*, discusses the process of developing a spiritual autobiography.

A Select Bibliography

Books About Journaling

Kelsey, Morton T. *Adventure Inward: Christian Growth Through Personal Journal Writing*. Minneapolis, MN: Augsburg Publishing House, 1980.

Klug, Ronald. *How to Keep a Spiritual Journal*. Nashville, TN: Thomas Nelson Publishers, 1982.

Progoff, Ira. *At a Journal Workshop: The Basic Text and Guide for Using the Intensive Journal*. New York: Dialogue House Library, 1975.

Simons, George F. *Keeping Your Personal Journal*. New York: Paulist Press, 1978.

Solly, Richard, and Roseann Lloyd. *Journey Notes: Writing for Recovery and Spiritual Growth*. San Francisco: Harper & Row, Publishers, 1989.

Examples of Journals

Elliot, Jim. *The Journals of Jim Elliot*. Ed. by Elisabeth Elliot. Old Tappan, NJ: Revell, 1978.

Frank, Anne. *Diary of Anne Frank*. Garden City, NY: Doubleday, 1967.

Hammarskjöld, Dag. *Markings*. Trans. by W. H. Auden & Leif Sjoberg. London: Faber and Faber, 1964.

Kierkegaard, Søren. *The Journals of Søren Kierkegaard*. Trans. by Alexander Dru. London: Collins, Fontana Books, 1958.

Livingstone, David. *Livingstone's Private Journals (1851–1853)*. Ed. by I Schapera. Berkeley, CA: University of California Press, 1960.

Pascal, Blaise. *Pensées*. Trans. by W. F. Trotter. New York: The Modern Library, Random House, 1941.

Saint Augustine. *Confessions*. Trans. by Henry Chadwick. Oxford: Oxford University Press, 1992.

Thielicke, Helmut. *African Diary: My Search for Understanding*. Waco, TX: Word, 1974.

Wesley, John. *The Journals of John Wesley: A Selection*. Ed. by Elisabeth Jay. Oxford: Oxford University Press, 1987.

LEADER'S NOTES FOR THIS STUDY

THE ART OF LEADERSHIP

It's not difficult to be a small group leader. All you need is

- ❖ the willingness to lead,
- ❖ the commitment to read through all of the materials prior to the session,
- ❖ the sensitivity to others that will allow you to guide the discussion without dominating it, and
- ❖ the willingness to be used by God as a small group leader.

Here are some basic small group principles that will help you do your job:

Ask the questions: Let group members respond.

Guide the discussion: Ask follow-up questions (or make comments) that draw others into the discussion and keep the discussion going. For example, "John, how would you answer the question?" Or, "Anybody else have any insights into this question?"

Start and stop on time: If you don't, people may be hesitant to come again since they never know when they will get home.

Stick to the time allotted to each section: There is always more that can be said in response to any question. It's your job to make sure the discussion keeps moving from question to question. Remember: it's better to cut off discussion when it's going well than to let it die out.

Model answers to questions: Whenever you ask a question to which everyone is expected to respond (for example, a "Telling Our Stories" question as opposed to a Bible study question), you, as leader, should be the first person to respond. In this way you model

the right length—and appropriate level—of response.

Understand the intention of the following different kinds of questions:

- ❖ *Experience questions:* The aim is to cause people to recall past experiences and share these memories with the group. There are no right or wrong answers to these questions. They facilitate the group process by getting people to share their stories and to think about the topic.

- ❖ *Forced-choice questions:* Certain questions will be followed by a series of suggested answers (with check-boxes). Generally, there is no "correct" answer. Options aid group members and guide their responses.

- ❖ *Questions with multiple parts:* Sometimes a question is asked and then various aspects of it are listed below. Ask the group members to answer each of the sub-questions. Their answers, taken together, will answer the initial question.

Introduce each section: This may involve a brief overview of the focus, purpose, and topic of the new section and instructions on how to do the exercise.

Guide the exercises: A major portion of your job will be introducing the Journaling Exercise. This is the heart of the group experience. Make sure the group has heard and understood the information found in the "Journaling Method" section. Then go over the instructions under "Journaling Exercise." Make sure everyone understands what is expected. Guide the preparation process and invite the group to begin journaling on their own.

End the journaling process when time is up. (Details of how to lead each section follow.)

Comment: Occasionally bring into the discussion some useful information from your own study. Keep your comments brief. Don't allow yourself to become the "expert" to whom everyone turns for the "right answer."

PREPARING FOR THE FIRST SESSION

Deliver a copy of this book to each potential group member. Ask them to read "The Art of Journaling" (pages 97-103). This describes what a journal is, how to create and use a journal, and why it's helpful to journal in a small group.

Session One: Using a Journal to Capture Your History

The first session is very important. People who attend will be deciding whether they want to be a part of the group. So your aim as small group leader is to

❖ generate vision about this small group (so each person will want to continue),

❖ give people an overview of the series (so they know where they are headed),

❖ begin to build relationships (so that a sense of community starts to develop), and

❖ encourage people to commit to the small group (so everyone will return next week, and perhaps bring a friend!).

A good way to start a small group is to share a meal before the first session. Eating draws people together and breaks down barriers between them. The aim of the meal is to get to know one another. Structure the meal so that lots of conversation takes place.

Following the meal, be sure to do the first session in its totality (don't merely

talk about what you're going to do when the group starts). Your aim is to give everyone the experience of being a part of this small group.

Introduction

Welcome: Greet people and let them know you're glad they've come and you look forward to being with them for the next eight weeks.

Prayer: Pray briefly, thanking God for this group and asking him to guide your deliberations and sharing today. Ask God to help you all learn how to use a journal as an aid for spiritual growth.

Group process: Describe how the small group will function and what it will study. Discuss, specifically:

❖ *Theme:* The aim is to learn to use a journal as a tool for spiritual growth.

❖ *Experience:* Explain that each session begins with a brief time of sharing in which the topic is introduced through experiences that group members have had ("Telling our Stories"). Then you will investigate a particular method of journaling ("Journaling Method") and use that method during a time of individual journaling ("Journaling Exercise"). In the "Journal Sharing" time, you will discuss your experiences together, both in terms of process (what you learned about journaling) and outcome (what you learned about yourself).

❖ *Details:* Describe where you will meet, when, and how long each session will last.

❖ *Aims:* Share the aims of the group: each person's spiritual growth will be enhanced, and each will have discerned more clearly his or her spiritual pilgrimage.

Telling Our Stories

Give the group a minute to look over the questions.

Begin the sharing. As leader, you should be the first to answer each question. (This is true only for questions in this section. Generally you ask questions and let the group respond.) Go around the group and give each person a chance to respond to the first question. Do the same for each question until time is up for the exercise.

Question 1: Listen carefully to the various reasons that drew people to the group. This is the implicit agenda. These are the needs, hopes, and issues the group needs to deal with.

Question 2: There are two aims here: to help people remember their experiences of journaling, and to broaden their view of what a journal is. "Journal," as used here, means "a personal record of our past, oral or written."

Journaling Method

you will have to decide how to communicate the information in this section. This is the theory that underlies the "Journal Excrcise." you don't want to take a lot of time to share this material, but it is vital information that the group needs in order to understand the exercise that follows. Options for covering this material include:

❖ *Individual reading:* Give the group a few minutes to read the material on their own.
❖ *Leader presentation:* Read this material aloud while people follow along, or summarize the section briefly.
❖ *Homework:* Ask the group to prepare for each session by reading the material in this section before you meet.

Journaling Exercise

Go over the instructions. Make sure each person understands the nature of the exercise well enough to work effectively during the silent journaling period.

Explain the nature of the focusing exercise (see below). Since you will use this exercise to begin each period of journaling, take time to explain it adequately.

Preparation: The aim is for people to relax and focus on the subject at hand. Sometimes it takes a while for us to set aside other concerns ("Will I enjoy this group?" "How am I going to solve that problem at work?").

Focusing Exercise (Relaxation & Prayer)

Relaxation: Ask people to find a comfortable place to sit. Make sure everyone has pen and paper. Many people prefer to sit in a chair with both feet on the floor. Others like to curl up in a chair with a cushion.

Then, have people close their eyes and start to relax. Ask them to relax the muscles first in their legs, then their stomachs, then their arms, and then their throats. Relaxation of the throat is especially important since many people are tense here. Next, ask people to slow down their breathing by inhaling and exhaling slowly several times.

Prayer: While people's eyes are still closed, pray. Ask the Holy Spirit to guide the exercise, leading people to insights and memories that are important for them.

Ask God to protect each person from evil so that their reflections will direct them to God and that what they experience will be from God. Pray that the discussion which follows the journaling will bring insight, clarity, and fellowship.

The relaxation and prayer should take no more than a few minutes. The rest of the "Journaling Exercise" is then spent in silence. Each person will work in his or her journal.

Journal Sharing

There are three parts to this. In the first part, sharing focuses on the journaling process. It is important, especially in the first two or three sessions, to talk about method. Some people find journaling to be very easy. But others have difficulty "getting it right." Talking about doing the exercise is a way for each person to learn more about the art of journaling. You may want to reduce or even eliminate this part in later sessions in order to have more time for personal sharing.

In the second part, you come to the heart of journal sharing: telling your stories to one another, based on what you have discovered as a result of journaling. When the journaling goes well, people will be eager to share their findings. In fact, this will be your major problem as group leader: guiding the discussion so that everyone has time to share and no one dominates.

In the final part of this session, commit your discussion to God in prayer. Allow each person to share a request, then pray. There are various ways to do this.

❖ *Free prayer:* Ask people to pray as they feel led. As leader, keep track of each person's request so that when you conclude in prayer, you can remember the requests that haven't been prayed for yet.

❖ *Circle prayer:* Ask each person to pray for the person on his or her right. This will only work with a group that is comfortable with spontaneous prayer.

❖ *Written prayer:* After sharing requests, allow two minutes for everyone to compose a short prayer. This is useful for groups that are learning to pray aloud.

❖ *Conversational prayer:* Invite members to pray sentence prayers, to pray more than once, and to pray in such a way as to build on each other's prayers. Make your prayer a group conversation with God.

❖ *Leader prayer:* If time is short, you may want to close the session with prayer. Or you may ask someone else to do so (but be sure he or she is comfortable with praying aloud).

When you've decided on a format appropriate for your group, describe how you will pray together. Later on, you may want to change formats.

Journaling Assignment
Use the remaining time to go over the weekly assignment. Reinforce the fact that people will learn to journal by journaling. It is important to spend some time journaling between group sessions.

Discuss the challenge of finding time to journal. Ask a few people to share when they journal. Urge people to decide on specific times when they will journal.

Point out that their assignment is to continue to explore the Present Period as a way of identifying the elements of their current life.

Make it clear that each person will be given two minutes to share from his or her journal at the start of the next session.

Concluding Issues: Group Invitation
If your first session is a trial meeting, invite everyone to return next week. If you have room in the group (there are fewer than twelve people), encourage members to invite their friends. After week two, new people cannot join the group since each time a new person comes it is necessary to rebuild the sense of community. Ask people to turn to page 8 and read the small group ground rules. Explain that they will be asked to agree to these guidelines next time if they decide to continue with the group.

Session Two: Using a Journal to Understand the Present
Group Covenant
In the second session, it is important to discuss the ground rules for the group (see page 8). Give the group a few minutes to look over the small group ground rules. Discuss the ground rules. Make sure everyone is comfortable with them. End by going around the group and giving everyone an opportunity to agree to the final group covenant.

The basic outline for how to proceed in each of the two small group sessions in this chapter is given in the notes for session one. Refresh your memory for how the group works by going over those notes first and then looking below at the specific details for this session.

Telling Our Stories

This week you have an option. Since your group has been journaling during the week, you may wish to begin by allowing each person to share briefly one important insight he or she has gained as a result of his or her work. The advantage of beginning this way is to encourage people to journal during the week. Also, the insights will be fresh and pertinent. This is a great way for group members to get to know one another quickly. If you choose this option:

❖ Divide the time available for this exercise (15-20 minutes) by the number of people in the group. This defines the maximum amount of time each person can share. For example, if you have twenty minutes available, in a group of ten people each person would be able to share for two minutes.

❖ As leader, you should begin the sharing. Then go around the circle and let each person share. Watch the time and gently rein in group members who take too long to share.

❖ Allow anyone to say, "Pass," if that person does not wish to share.

You may choose, however, to use the exercise provided. Or you might combine both options, allowing time for brief sharing from journals and ending with one of the questions from the exercise. Since the focus of this session is on a Daily Log, the sharing exercise looks at how we organize our days, with emphasis on the pressures we face in our daily routines.

Journaling Method

Read or summarize the text to communicate the vital information in this section. Group members need to understand the concept of a Daily Log in order for them to do the Journaling Exercise successfully.

Journaling Exercise

Go over the instructions with the group. Make sure each person understands the exercise well enough to work effectively during the silent journaling period. Start the focusing exercise, and help people to relax. Pray for God's guidance and protection. Invite the group to journal in silence and to follow the instructions in the text.

Journal Sharing

Discuss both the process of journaling (what was learned about this journal method) and the results of journaling (new insights into the lives of group members). End with a time of focused prayer about the issues that emerged during the sharing.

Journaling Assignment

Use the final few minutes to go over the weekly assignment.

Session Three: Using a Journal to Recover Your Past

Telling Our Stories

The focus of the Journaling Exercise will be on recovering our past. The questions in this section will help the group remember some of the good times that happened "back then." The questions concentrate on seeing life as a series of time frames, each with its own distinctive character.

Journaling Exercise

The numbers are important—they divide life into the right amount of periods. With fewer than eight periods, you will explore time frames that are too long; with more than twelve, the time frames are too short.

Journal Sharing

In part one, ask about the ease or difficulty in identifying eight to twelve hinge events. For some people, such a list comes easily and spontaneously; for others, it's a much more difficult exercise. Assure people that whatever list they came up with will suffice as a way to define the structure of their past.

Begin the second part by asking two or three people to read their list of hinge events. Then you might ask others to identify some of the hinge events they found. Ask which periods captured their attention and why.

By now you realize how important the prayer time is. Prayer that is based on deep personal insight is a powerful experience. Be sure to leave plenty of time for prayer. You will probably find that the group needs more and more time for prayer as the weeks go by.

Session Four: Using a Journal to Interact with Your History
Telling Our Stories
The focus in the Journaling Exercise will be on interacting with people through the process of dialogue. This exercise encourages people to think about friendship.

It will be interesting to compare what people consider the key characteristic of a good friend to be. This list could be used to critique what kinds of friends we are. Which characteristic describes how we relate as a friend to others?

Journaling Method
Journal dialogues will be unfamiliar to some people and downright strange to others. Encourage people to suspend their doubts until they try it. The experience itself is usually enough to convince most people of the value of journal dialogue. For those who remain unconvinced, there is no need for them to pursue this method any further. There are many other ways for them to work in their journals.

Journaling Exercise
Since this is a multi-part exercise, be sure to allow plenty of time.

One of the instructions is to read the

journal dialogue aloud when it is complete. This is not possible when journaling in a group, so ask people to read it silently. Later on, when they are alone, people can read their entries aloud.

Journal Sharing
Be sure to discuss the process of journaling since this is a new kind of exercise. Some people may have had difficulty with it, so the group's help will be useful.

Session Five: Using a Journal to Realize Your Future
Telling Our Stories
What we actually become is something different from our dreams in childhood and high school. It is a mix of training, circumstances, networking, social needs, and economics. Still, sometimes you will find important paths for the future buried in past plans. Maybe that little boy who wanted to be a fireman will join the auxiliary police, become an EMT, and work on an ambulance two nights a week, or even join a volunteer fire department—thus fulfilling the desire to help others in emergencies.

Journaling Method
Three journal methods are touched upon here. However, they are variations on a single theme: understanding future directions. The main exercise focuses on crossroads experiences and discerning whether the road not taken still needs to be explored. A variation on that exercise suggests that if a person is at a crossroads right now, he or she should try to imagine where various paths might take him or her. The remaining exercise, Patterns, is described only briefly. It is a natural extension of the work that's been done with different periods. Suggest that the group try the Patterns exercise during the week.

Journaling Exercise and Journal Sharing
By now you have established a regular pattern with the group. Continue with what you've been doing.

110

Session Six: Using a Journal to Explore Your Emotional Responses

Telling Our Stories

The questions will help group members to explore their creative side. Many of us don't view ourselves as creative. Hence it is important to discover the ways in which we are.

Journaling Exercise and Journal Sharing

Either exercise will yield useful insights.

Session Seven: Using a Journal to Nurture Your Spiritual Life

Telling Our Stories

To address the question of spiritual life, you must begin with each person's experience of and relationship to God. These questions facilitate this sort of conversation.

Question 3: An experience of God is one thing; responding to God is another. Often the experience of God's presence causes us to commit our lives to God. Conversion experiences (turning to God in repentance and faith in Jesus) happen in a variety of ways. The question is purposely vague. It does not seek to define a conversion experience. It is really asking for a recollection of events in life when a person shifts direction because of conviction and because God intervenes in some way. This can happen suddenly (as it did to the apostle Paul) or gradually (as it did to the other twelve apostles). While conversion to Christianity is a singular event, we experience many kinds of God-directed conversions over the course of our lives, both large and small shifts that move us in a God-ward direction. Let group members recall their conversions. If you run out of time, suggest that people use their journals to recall "conversions" they have had.

Next Session

Next week's exercise will focus on studying the Bible, so ask people to bring along Bibles—whole Bibles and not just New Testaments since you will work with a passage from the Old Testament. (you will probably want to bring along extra Bibles because people may forget.)

Session Eight: Using a Journal to Reflect on the Bible

Journaling Method

Make sure everyone has a Bible. You can't study the text if you do not have the text! Bring extra copies of the Bible with you.

The method to be followed is straightforward, with potential problems coming at two points—selection of the passage, and getting through the passage. It is good to cover the entire book of Ruth if you can so try to get someone to look at each set of questions. However, don't press too much since the crucial thing is not that you touch on each text but that each person makes important connections to the text. Help people to use their journaling time wisely. It is easy to get so involved in one of the three questions that you do not get to the others. It is important that people respond to each of the three questions.

Journal Sharing

It will be up to you to lead the discussion on what next step the group should take. There are various options.

❖ *Spiritual Autobiography: Discovering and Sharing Your Spiritual Story*: This study guide presents the next logical step now that you have learned how to journal.

❖ *Journaling group*: Continue to journal together, reading portions of your journals together, discussing insights gleaned, and praying for one another.

❖ *Bible study*: Start a Bible study group together in which you explore a book or topic in the Bible.

If you enjoyed SPIRITUAL JOURNALING, you'll want to explore the rest of this series as well.

Spiritual disciplines are simply ways to open ourselves to God. They help us become aware of the many ways God speaks to us and provide us with ways to respond. SPIRITUAL FORMATION study guides by Richard Peace explore and explain how the use of disciplines (such as journaling, Bible reading, and prayer) can deepen both our walk with God and our community with other believers. While many think of the spiritual disciplines as solitary pursuits, this series allows group members to share together the riches of a deeper walk with God.

Other Spiritual Formation study guides by Richard Peace include:

Contemplative Bible Reading
Meditative Prayer
Spiritual Autobiography

NAVPRESS

BRINGING TRUTH TO LIFE